c/??c

FAST DECISIONS:
Think Fast. Be Bold.
Be Fearless.

Master Confidence in Chaos – Make Decisions Under Pressure

By:

Dr. Geoffrey Mount Varner

This book is a work of nonfiction. The information and advice contained in the book are based upon the research, and the personal and professional experiences of the author:

Copyright © 2025 by Dr. Geoffrey Mount Varner

Edited by Georgina Chong-You

Frst Paperback Edition

ISBN: 978-0-9980336-1-7

Printed in the United States of America

Thank You.

You could've picked any book—but you chose this one. That tells me something about you: You want to move faster, decide bolder, and live fearlessly. You're not waiting for permission. You're ready to take control, lead in chaos, and make the hard calls that others avoid.

Thank you for showing up. Let's move.

Decision-making - *the act of choosing a course of action from various options to achieve a goal. It involves evaluating alternatives, weighing risks, and committing to a choice with a decisive purpose.*

Fast decision-making *–the ability to swiftly assess a situation, evaluate options, and make a confident choice under time pressure, driven by a mindset of optimal clarity and focus. It requires the development of mental readiness to act decisively and adapt quickly.*

Table of Contents

Introduction

My Story

Every reason or response has a story that precedes it. Here's mine...

What if I told you that your ability to make fast decisions could one day save your life? What if hesitation—whether weeks, days or even hours—meant the difference between life and death?

As a decision-making expert, I've spent decades thinking fast, being bold, and making critical choices under pressure. But nothing prepared me for the day those skills became the reason I'm still alive today.

Most people don't realize how dangerous hesitation can be—until it's too late. We assume we have time to weigh our options and carefully consider every detail. But life doesn't always give us that luxury. When the pressure is intense, and the stakes are high, the question isn't whether you'll decide—it's whether you'll choose fast to enough to make a difference.

> *The difference between succeeding and failing, winning and losing—even life and death—comes down to one thing: how fast you decide.*

As an emergency medicine physician for over 25 years, I have mastered making fast, decisive choices in the most critical moments. These high-pressure scenarios include managing mass casualties, treating patients who were acutely injured and ill patients in the ER, directing medical operations for a presidential inauguration, the medical director responsible for the emergency response to Ebola, shaping government strategies during the COVID-19 pandemic and responding to international outbreaks.

These aren't just professional experiences—they've shaped who I am. I've applied the same precision and urgency as a business executive, a husband, and a father. Over these two decades, I've developed unique skills related to swift decision-making. I'll begin with a personal story showing how making optimal fast decisions saved my life.

In February of 2023, at age 56, I noticed that I had been waking up to urinate about six to seven times every night. My daytime urination was even more frequent than at night. I decided to schedule an appointment with my primary care doctor.

A week later, I was sitting in his office. After a few clinical questions, the doctor recommended a prostatic-specific antigen test, known as a PSA—a blood test that screens for prostate cancer. The results returned the same day and showed a PSA level of 4.0 ng/ml. The normal range is between 0 and 4 ng/ml, higher than my previous result a year earlier, so my doctor referred me to a urologist. Without hesitation, I scheduled the appointment with the urologist and was seen on March 2. Given my symptoms and concerns, the urologist recommended a follow-up visit for a biopsy. I agreed and rearranged my schedule for the first available biopsy appointment on March 11.

For prostate biopsies, they usually do 12-core samples to evaluate under the microscope for cancer. A few weeks later, the biopsy revealed no pathology in the samples, and everything was normal. I was excited and knew I would not need another biopsy for a while.

In early August, I noticed an intermittent bulge in my inguinal area—just inside of my right hip. I quickly scheduled an appointment with a surgeon for August 22. The surgeon diagnosed me with a hernia that needed to be repaired surgically. He said I could wait a few months for the repair or do it sooner. The following week, I completed the procedure as quickly as possible.

As part of the pre-operative procedure, routine labs were done, and I asked to have a PSA included. The doctor said my biopsy a few months ago was normal, and there was no need, but he ordered it anyway at my request. When the lab results came back, I was told that I was cleared for surgery, though his surgeon's office didn't tell him the actual lab results, and for some reason, I was not able to open my electronic medical records to review the results myself.

After the procedure, I could not open my chart, so I contacted the surgeon and asked him to send me the labs. That's when I discovered the current PSA—taken months after the previous one—was 11.2 ng/ml, nearly three times higher than usual.

I immediately scheduled a new appointment with my urologist. It was now October of 2023. The urologist thought the dramatic rise in his PSA level was caused by prostatitis, which is an infected or inflamed prostate or a urinary tract infection. I was treated with antibiotics for the infection, but to be sure it wasn't cancer, the urologist asked me to schedule an appointment for an MRI in the near future. When I left the office, I scheduled an MRI for as soon as an appointment was available, which was on October 17.

After I'd completed the antibiotics, I took another PSA. It was still high at 9.1 ng/ml. The MRI revealed "chronic prostatitis" and a high likelihood of prostate cancer.

The urologist was hopeful that chronic prostatitis could explain the MRI results, but he wanted to be sure. So, he recommended another biopsy as soon as I could clear my schedule—but no longer than two to three months. I quickly cleared my schedule, and the biopsy was done two weeks later, on November 10th.

My fast decisions thus far:

1. Scheduling the hernia surgery as soon as possible versus waiting a few months—this decision led to the early discovery of an elevated PSA.

2. Scheduling the first appointment with the urologist as soon as he was available.

3. I decided to have the MRI done faster than expected and did not assume that the elevated PSA was due to an infection.

4. Scheduling the second biopsy as soon as possible—two weeks—even after hearing the "within two to three months" suggestion.

On December 4th, I walked into the urologist's office, fully expecting the second biopsy results to confirm what I had been hoping for—no cancer. But the doctor's expression quickly erased any sense of reassurance. With a steady, serious tone, he informed me that I had malignant adenocarcinoma of the prostate. He explained that some prostate cancers progress so slowly that they can initially be monitored, a process known as "active surveillance." However, my case was different. The doctor was clear: "This is not a cancer we can afford to wait on. You need treatment very soon."

He outlined several treatment options, each with its own set of implications. However, before proceeding, he emphasized the importance of obtaining a positron emission tomography (PET) scan, a specialized imaging test, to determine whether the cancer had spread beyond the prostate.

I could barely hold back my tears as I went to the front desk to schedule my next appointment. When I got to my car, I cried alone, went home, and decided *not* to tell family and friends until I had more information. The next day was back to making decisions. The next in this series of decisions was to find out where I could get the PET scan done soon. I then needed to do quick, not extensive, research and find out which were the best hospitals for treating prostate cancer.

The PET scan results did not show any evidence of spread, and thus, chemo would not be needed.

Yet, I still had to decide about treatment options—the possibilities included radiation, hormonal suppression, conventional surgery, intensity-modulated radiation, cryosurgery, high-intensity focused ultrasound (HIFU), and a few others. The urologist did share with me that because of the grade of prostate cancer, my age, and based on all the results thus far, surgical removal of the prostate would be my best option.

Choosing not to stop there. I conducted my own research and immediately sought a second opinion. Timing was critical, and I saw a renowned urologist just before he left for a month-long vacation. His assessment echoed the first: surgery was the best and most urgent course of action. His parting words stayed with me as he left: *"Don't let anyone convince you otherwise. Time is not on your side."*

This doctor's advice was unmistakably clear and urgent—**I needed to act fast**. Since my initial urologist no longer did surgery, I immediately sought an appointment with the top prostate surgeon specializing in radical nerve-sparing robotic prostatectomies. However, I was met with a serious barrier: a five to six-month wait just for an initial consultation. Knowing time was critical, I quickly made several phone calls and mobilized my network without hesitation, calling on every connection I had. I was able to be seen the following week.

The surgeon's staff gave me a range of dates for surgery, and I chose the soonest one. The surgery took place on February 14, 2024, and went extremely well. I elected to go home from the hospital a day earlier than recommended, believing that being with my family would be more likely to aid in my healing process than staying in a hospital room.

I talked to the surgeon after the procedure. He said, "I reviewed your entire chart, and you had so much done so quickly. Deciding to have surgery so soon after the diagnosis was quite impressive and likely saved your life. I have patients I diagnosed over a year ago who are still deciding."

I returned to work sooner than expected.

A summary of fast decisions:

1. I sought out a place that could do the PET scan immediately.

2. I quickly sought the opinion of the second urologist and pushed to get an appointment before this man went on vacation.

3. While many people take weeks or months to weigh the many treatment options, I decided to have the surgery within a week.

4. I pulled some strings to get an appointment with a prostate surgeon who was usually booked for months.

5. I chose and pushed for the earliest available date when given a range of available dates.

The series of fast decisions enabled me to be treated about twelve to thirteen months sooner than someone without fast decision-making skills.

My recovery

The weeks after surgery tested me in ways I couldn't have anticipated. I had six fresh incisions in my abdomen, two of which appeared infected. I couldn't eat, and the indwelling urinary catheter in my penis caused sharp pain with even the slightest movement. And things got more interesting. I started to question: Did I make the right decision? Should I have chosen radiation? Should I have gone to a different hospital? The doubts weren't just mine—friends, acquaintances, even strangers chimed in: *"Why didn't you wait? Prostate cancer is slowly growing. Why surgery at all?"*

These questions lingered as my recovery was more challenging than expected. Weeks later, after the catheter was removed, I faced a new hurdle: incontinence. I vividly remember standing in a grocery store when urine began leaking for no reason. I froze in embarrassment, unable to stop it. My abdominal muscles spasmed violently, a side effect of the surgery, and my weight plummeted because I couldn't eat. My incisions healed poorly, leaving me physically and mentally drained.

But that ordeal taught me that decisions don't end when you make them. Decision-making is a skill—a pliable, ever-evolving process. When a choice doesn't lead to the outcome you hoped for, you don't stop. You *decide again*. And again. Every challenge requires another option, another action. Recovery wasn't just about healing my body; it was about recommitting to my decisions and moving forward with unwavering focus, no matter how tough the road ahead.

The aftereffects of my surgery brought an unexpected gift: **clarity**. As my life slowed down, so did the world around me. My thoughts sharpened, and I began connecting this experience with countless others from my past. Concepts that once felt abstract—mindset, confidence, fear, managing your nerves, neuroplasticity, and the ability to make one decision after another no matter what—became strikingly vivid. Something I'd written about extensively suddenly revealed itself in ways I had never fully articulated before.

Lying under the covers just hours after surgery and then again on many sleepless nights during recovery, I saw with absolute clarity the process of mastering the factors of fast decision-making. This life-or-death experience was more than a challenge—it was a revelation, offering profound insights into the art of quick decision-making.

I'm opening this book with this story because it captures something vital: the extraordinary, life-changing, and even life-saving power of making fast decisions in the face of uncertainty. I have lived this lesson, and I hope it will inspire and guide others when they face their own critical moments.

How and Why I Wrote This Book

In July 2020, during the height of the COVID pandemic, I was in the middle of one of hundreds of national and international TV and radio interviews. One host posed a simple yet powerful question: "How do I make better and faster decisions?" At that moment, I realized this wasn't just a passing curiosity—it was a universal challenge.

This question echoed what colleagues, students, residents, family, and others had asked me for years, particularly during the speaking tour for my previous book, *Training Your Mind for Split-Second Decisions*. That book focused on decisions made in seconds or less—often in emergencies, where lives hung in the balance. But this host's question highlighted something different: the critical need for a resource to guide people in making fast, effective decisions in everyday life—decisions made with slightly more time, especially when the situation is anticipated.

From the countless conversations I've had relating to making fast, effective decisions, a clear set of needs emerged—needs that inspired this book:

- ❖ A practical method to make decisions quickly and effectively.

- ❖ Skills to build confidence in decision-making under pressure.

- ❖ Strategies to develop a stronger, more resilient mindset.

- ❖ Tools to manage *fear* when faced with tough choices.

- ❖ Techniques to persevere when a decision doesn't yield the desired outcome.

This book isn't just a guide; it's a roadmap to making bold, life-defining decisions with confidence and clarity.

Whether you're navigating the chaos of a crisis or the complexity of everyday challenges, the tools and strategies in these pages will equip you to move forward with clarity, confidence, and purpose.

How this book will benefit you

In the first chapter, we will begin the process of increasing self-confidence and improving mindset. I will include relevant information from neuroscience, psychology, medicine, and other fields.

- ❖ You will learn that confidence is a skill to be developed and how to use that skill.

- ❖ You will learn to adjust your mindset so that it maximally benefits you and your decision-making.

- ❖ You will learn to identify, manage, and move past fear.

- ❖ You will be a better decision maker, and even under time pressure, you will be an improved optimal decision maker.

The book's backdrop will use the four-step framework of fast decision-making – time, information, consequences, and decisions. You will understand why too much information can interfere with or slow decision-making. You will learn how decision-making under pressure and time can cause different cognitive biases and heuristics to impact your fast decisions.

Before my prostate cancer journey, I had already developed the concept of fast decision-making under pressure. I understood that mindset plays a pivotal role in directing your choices, especially when you don't have all the necessary knowledge or information. But the experience of navigating cancer changed my understanding. It revealed something critical: the terrain of decision-making is constantly shifting. Adapting to that ever-changing environment and making faster, more decisive choices became essential—to survive and thrive.

One key revelation is the unpredictable nature of fear. Fear doesn't politely announce itself; it strikes suddenly and often at the worst moments. Managing that fear, staying calm, and moving forward anyway became non-negotiable. While I already valued confidence, this experience deepened my understanding of its importance. Confidence isn't static—it must be cultivated daily, especially when decisions don't lead to the outcomes you'd hoped for. Building personal confidence became a discipline, a skill to be mastered and maintained.

My journey clarified this profound truth: our time on earth is finite. Every moment spent hesitating is a moment lost. The faster you make decisions, the faster you align your actions with your mindset, goals, and values. The sooner you decide, the sooner you can reap the rewards of those decisions and enjoy the life you're working toward.

This isn't just about making decisions—it's about living with urgency, clarity, and purpose. The faster you decide, the more time you have to embrace the results and truly live.

How to Use This Book

Not all decisions are created equal, and there's more than one way to make them. However, having a flexible framework to adapt to your style will make you an unstoppable decision-maker. This book will give you the tools to make faster, better decisions and elevate both your personal and professional life.

Think about elite athletes—what sets them apart? Reps. They practice more than their peers, mastering the skills that lead to excellence. The same principle applies to decision-making. The more you practice the key elements—mindset, confidence, managing fear—the sharper and more effective your decisions become.

Here's how to get the most out of this book:

1. **Read it from start to finish.** Commit to understanding the concepts before diving into the exercises.

2. **Revisit the chapters that resonate most.** Focus on the exercises that stand out to you. Commit to one exercise for two weeks, then move on to the next.

3. **Practice consistently in low-stakes environments.** Make decisions in everyday situations to refine your skills. This will ensure that you're fully prepared for high-stakes decisions.

4. **Track Your Progress.** Keep a journal to log your decisions and reflect on your outcomes. Write down what worked, what didn't, and what you learned. This habit creates a feedback loop, helping you measure growth and identify areas for improvement.

5. **Apply What You Learn to Real-World Scenarios.** Use the frameworks and exercises in actual decisions, starting with smaller choices and progressing to high-stakes

situations. Consistently applying these strategies will build your confidence, speed, and precision under pressure.

Commit to the process, put in the reps, and watch your decision-making skills transform. The more you invest, the greater your confidence and results.

What Is a Fast Decision?

Fast decisions are crucial choices made under intense time pressure with significant consequences, regardless of whether information is limited or plentiful. Though swift, these decisions are not always instantaneous, allowing for some consideration of options at times. Whatever you think is the right amount of time to make a fast decision, I want to encourage you to decide faster than that. Decide faster because in critical moments, hesitation is the enemy of success.

Fast decisions occur in various contexts, such as business crises, medical emergencies, parenting dilemmas, financial investments, relationships, and everyday interactions. The consequences are sometimes life and death and, at times, may change the trajectory of your life. More often, the stakes are high but not life-or-death, as in a situation where you make a successful or unsuccessful investment.

In short, significant, fast decisions are critical choices made under intense time pressure with substantial consequences, and often with incomplete information.

Fast decision-making is a multifaceted process that requires mental preparation, clarity under pressure, and strategic thinking. By learning and practicing the techniques I will share with you in this book, you can improve your mindset and mental resilience, thereby improving your ability to make fast, effective decisions, even in the face of uncertainty. The ability to make fast decisions is not just a skill; it's a mindset that can be developed and honed over time.

As an ER doctor, executive, father, mass casualty expert, and decisions expert, fast decisions are a fundamental part of my job. I've trained for them and have trained thousands of others in their decision-making.

While ER doctors make faster decisions than most people, you will face at least one instance where making a fast decision will have a significant impact personally, professionally, or socially. It is vital for you to be prepared for the decisions that you know are coming. With rapid advancements in technology and new diseases on the horizon, our world is moving faster and faster. Decisions must also come faster, and decisiveness will win the day.

Entrepreneurs swamped with decisions, team leaders pushing large organizations forward, and executives who've scaled the heights of leadership through keen critical thinking—yet find themselves hesitating or seeking consensus—will find actionable and life-changing insights within these pages.

If you are a parent making quick decisions for your family's well-being, a college student facing a whirlwind of choices coming at you faster than ever, or a sharp-witted adolescent learning to make the right calls in each new situation, this guide will also help you.

By mastering fast decision-making, you can create the life you've always dreamed of—achieving the career, relationships, and lifestyle you deserve. The choices you make today, whether about leaving a job, ending a marriage, growing your family, or creating cherished memories, are steps toward the life you are meant to live. The sooner you make both easy and tough decisions, the sooner you will get to the life that you have a right to live.

Tomorrow is a bonus - Decide as if your life depended on it

The one absolute truth that we all come to recognize is that our time on earth is limited. And what you have done from your earliest years to the day you die rests on your decisions. To put it another way—you are the product of your decisions. Have you ever wondered why some people appear to accomplish in one lifetime what it would take many multiple lifetimes for others to accomplish? It comes down to their ability to make decisions. One of the most important reasons to learn to make a fast decision is that doing so allows you to move on to the next decision. The more you hesitate, the more you prevent yourself from tackling the next problem. Also, small decisions lead to bigger decisions. And bigger decisions lead to bigger consequences. As in the introductory story that led to life-saving surgery, achieving your goals usually requires a series of decisions, each building on the previous. That is why it is so important to practice improving our decision-making skills consistently. Expertise in any area is about repetition and improving your skills. Fast decision-making is the same way.

What many of us experience is that time pressure—feeling squeezed by the clock, feeling there aren't enough hours in the day to tackle the heap of work *and* make those big calls—can throw off our thinking, mess with our ability to figure out what to do first, and hinder our effectiveness. Time pressure increases our stress, disrupting our capacity to decide swiftly and act. And yet, frustratingly, time-pressure situations are exactly when you need to decide fast and think fast. One of the premises of this book is that if you practice a set of decision-making skills repeatedly in hypothetical or low-pressure situations, you will have the muscle memory to make effective decisions when the stakes are high and the time is short.

I acknowledge that a decision can have a lasting impact on your own life and others' lives, too. That understandably causes many people to struggle with even the simplest choices. That is why we're building a robust framework, guiding you from the basics of decision-making through complex, highly consequential decisions.

By the end of this book, you will be able to make fast decisions that previously seemed daunting. Read the book, follow the steps, and you'll emerge empowered and confident. Be bold, be decisive, and let's turn the page together.

Chapter One:

The Decisions Mindset

A craven hung along the battle's edge,
And thought, 'Had I a sword keener steel-
That blue blade the king's son bears - but this blunt thing-!'
And lowering crept away and left the field.
Then came the king's son, wounded, sore bestead.
And weaponless, and saw the broken sword,
And ran and snatched it, and with battle-shout.
Lifted afresh, he hewed his enemy down,
And saved a great cause that heroic day.
—from "Opportunity" by Edward Rowland Sill

E verything starts and ends with your mindset. Your mindset is not just a concept; it's the immovable foundation of your life. Mindset is the core beliefs and values you hold about yourself, and it dictates how you think, perceive, and interact with the world. Your mindset isn't passive—it's the lens through which you interpret every situation, beat challenges, and take advantage of opportunities. It defines your actions, shapes your outcomes, and determines your destiny.

Exercise:

I want to challenge you to do something the next time you go to the grocery store. You are going to start your training now. We will make small decisions under the pressure of time when the stakes are low. Here is the first drill:

1. Create a list of 10 items that you need from the grocery store

1. **Set a Timer**: Give yourself 15 minutes to get all the necessary items. The timer starts when you walk into the store and stops when you leave.

2. **Checkout Line Option**: You can choose to stop the timer when you get to the checkout line, but you can't stop it and then go back for more items.

3. **Prioritize**: Focus on getting the most important items first since you might not get everything on your list.

4. **No Return**: After the exercise, go home without returning to the store to get missed items.

5. **Build Confidence**: This practice helps you prioritize, builds confidence, and reduces fear over time. You'll realize that life goes on even if you miss some items.

This practice will gradually build your confidence by helping to reduce fear. When you don't get the exact results you hoped for, and yet life carries on, you understand that you're still fine even when decisions don't go as planned. The world doesn't end. Many people hesitate to make decisions, fearing mistakes and their consequences, but with practice, you'll find that this fear starts to fade.

Building confidence in fast decision-making is a habit, and like any habit, it requires repetition. The more you practice making quick choices, the more momentum you'll gain, and the stronger your confidence will become. Matthew 9:29 says, "According to your faith, be it unto you." Your faith—your mindset—decides what you achieve, not chance and not circumstance. The truth is absolute.

How you see the world is exactly how it will be. The input of your thoughts is everything because what you put in determines what you get out. Your thoughts are not just whimsical ideas—they are the raw material that creates your mindset, and your mindset dictates your entire experience of life.

If your life isn't what you want, your mindset isn't where it needs to be. Change it. Take control. Feed your mind with intention, think with purpose, and act with absolute conviction. Your world will not change until you do; the power to make that change is yours.

Adopt a Growth Mindset

Your mindset is built on your beliefs about yourself and the world, formed through your experiences—both successes and failures. Researchers identify two primary types of mindsets: fixed and growth.

A **fixed mindset** is a mental prison. People with a fixed mindset believe they are stuck as they are—their abilities, intelligence, and talents are unchangeable. They avoid challenges, fear failure, and quit at the first sign of resistance. They justify mediocrity with excuses like:

- ❖ "I'm not good at writing, so there's no point in improving."

- ❖ "I tried starting a business once and failed, so I'm not trying again."

- ❖ "I'm overweight—it's just my body type, and there's nothing I can do."

- ❖ "I applied for a promotion and didn't get it. I guess I'll stay where I am."

These statements are not truths but excuses rooted in fear and complacency. People with a fixed mindset sabotage their own potential by surrendering to the first setback and refusing to try again. They settle, stop, and fail—because they choose to.

> *In critical moments, hesitation is the enemy of success.*

But this does not have to be your story. Your mindset is yours to control.

Adopt a growth mindset—no hesitation, no excuses. Every challenge is an opportunity, every failure a lesson, and every day a chance to rise. This is not optional; it's an absolute choice: master your mindset or let it control you. The world does not reward the passive or the complacent—it rewards those who take control, persist, and refuse to quit. Decide now to grow. No one will do it for you.

Those with a growth mindset know they can learn, achieve, and become anything. There is no ceiling, no limit—only what they decide to reach for. They see challenges as opportunities, not obstacles. No matter how hard the path or how many times they fall, they persist because they believe in their ability to succeed or learn what's necessary. They don't fear criticism; they embrace it. The growth mindset says, "I didn't win this time, but I will next time," or "You got me once, but you won't get me again." This mindset doesn't stop, it doesn't retreat—it moves forward, always.

Your mindset is the ultimate determining factor in what you can or cannot do. As it's been said, "The person who thinks they can and the person who thinks they can't are both correct." Your belief in your potential—your mindset—is the most significant force shaping your future.

Thoughts are not fleeting; they are creative forces that shape your reality. Everything about your current circumstances— whether you're thriving or struggling—directly results from your thoughts. Your income, relationships, education, and status are all manifestations of the beliefs and ideas you've held onto in the past. This truth is non-negotiable: where you are today is the sum of your past thoughts and decisions.

This may be hard to accept, but it's true nonetheless: you are responsible for your reality. While there are exceptions like serious crimes or mass tragedies, the overwhelming majority of what happens in your life stems from the thoughts you feed your mind. Your habitual thoughts are the engine driving your life.

Mindset and Decision-Making

Joseph Murphy stated in *The Power of Your Subconscious Mind*, "You have a mind, and you must learn to master it." Your mind operates on two levels—the conscious, which thinks, and the subconscious, which creates. Your conscious mind chooses your thoughts, and whatever you believe consistently sinks into your subconscious, transforming those thoughts into reality. This process is not optional; it is absolute. The subconscious is the seat of your emotions and the source of your creativity, and it works relentlessly, whether you feed it positive or negative thoughts. What you think, you create.

Here's the undeniable truth: once your subconscious accepts an idea, it executes it with unwavering precision. In turn, you will have the confidence to make fast decisions no matter the circumstance. This law does not discriminate—positive, constructive thinking results in health, success, and prosperity. Negative, destructive thinking invites failure, frustration, and unhappiness. This is not a suggestion; it is an immutable law. Your habitual thoughts, whether empowering or harmful, dictate the quality of your life. Period.

If your mind is filled with fear, doubt, and worry, you are programming your subconscious to create exactly what you fear. For instance, if you obsessively worry about your purse being stolen, you are directing your subconscious to attract that scenario into your life. The subconscious doesn't judge or question; it executes. It simply gives you what you feed it—good or bad. You cannot escape this truth. Your mind is the ultimate creator of your reality. If your life isn't where you want it to be, the problem is clear: you are feeding your subconscious the wrong thoughts. Change it. Take absolute control of your thinking. Discipline your conscious mind to think only constructive, harmonious thoughts. Fill your mind with clarity, focus, and purpose; your subconscious will follow suit, creating your desired life.

If you take only one thing from this message, let it be this: your thoughts are creative. You are not a victim of circumstance—you are the architect of your life. The life you live today directly reflects the thoughts you've consistently entertained. Your habitual thoughts have the most profound impact on your reality.

Habitual thoughts are automatic mental patterns and beliefs you think repeatedly, often without conscious awareness. They dominate your mind regularly, shaping how you perceive and respond to the world. Over time, they become ingrained in your subconscious, influencing your actions, emotions, and overall life outcomes.

Habitual thoughts are the patterns that govern your emotions, actions, and your destiny. These patterns either serve you—or destroy you. Recognize this truth and take control. The process is not passive; it demands intention, awareness, and persistence. Identify the thoughts that do not serve you and eliminate them. Replace them with thoughts aligned with the reality you want to create. The power of thought goes beyond what we can see or touch. It is metaphysical energy in its purest form. Your habitual thoughts emit vibrations that attract people, opportunities, and outcomes that match their frequency.

Your life is not controlled by what people say to you, how they treat you, or what they have done to you. You control your universe with your thoughts. Shakespeare wrote, "There is nothing good or bad, but thinking makes it so." This is not poetry; it is fact. That is why learning to have habitual thoughts that elevate you is so important. The transformation process is deliberate and requires effort, but it is within your power to start today.

The key is already in your hands, and that key is your mind. Decide now to elevate your thoughts. Think with intention. Act with purpose. Positive, empowering thoughts attract success and abundance. Negative, destructive thoughts invite chaos and failure. Therefore, what you think about consistently, you manifest. Now let's try some thought exercises:

Exercise 1: Notice Your Habitual Thoughts

Here are a few concrete steps to help you identify your habitual thoughts and begin to change them.

a) Set your phone alarm to ring four to five random times a day for a week.

b) Each time the alarm sounds, pause and reflect on your current thoughts, and write down in one or two sentences what you were thinking.

c) At the end of the week, read over your notes. You will find patterns.

d) Organize all the thoughts you've written down into two main categories: positive and negative.

The good news is simply noticing your thoughts is a step in the right direction. The next step is to change them.

Exercises 2–8: Change Your Habitual Thoughts

1. **Awake, Appreciate, and Sleep**, Appreciate. Before you step out of bed each morning and after you get in bed at night, think about five things you are grateful for. These must be things that have happened in the last 24 hours or will happen in the next 24 hours. It can be as simple as,

   - "I am grateful that I'm about to have a cup of coffee,"

   - "I am grateful that I have a great book that I am reading,"

   - "I am grateful that I have a job," even if you don't like your job now.

   This practice lets you start your day in the morning with a thought pattern aligned with optimistic energy, leading to constructive thoughts and a more positive day. Sleep is a restorative and healing period. Hence, at night, having thoughts steeped in appreciation prepares and attunes your subconscious for a more peaceful sleep. Your mind will be refueling with constructive energy because of how it transitioned into sleep.

2. **Morning Practice:** positive thoughts. At breakfast, take a moment to focus on positive thoughts. This requires a mindful effort. For example, if you have a task you are struggling with or don't want to do, instead of saying, "I do

not want to...," say, "I get to...." This slight language change sends a positive signal to your brain. Other phrases you can use include:

- "Today is up to me; make it a great day."

- "Today is full of possibilities, and I have the power to make it a great day."

- "I will spread kindness and positivity to those around me."

3. **Meditate daily:** Meditation is the practice of calming and centering your mind. You can focus intensely on a specific concept or idea or simply still your mind and become aware of meditating. If you focus your thoughts on a concept, you will begin to understand and embody this concept more deeply. This concept will integrate into your identity, becoming a part of your identity. So, if you meditate on positive, uplifting, compassionate, and kind thoughts, these qualities will gradually be reflected in your character. Change or transformation is a daily journey requiring consistent practice and dedication. As a man thinketh, so he is.

4. **Substitute positive thoughts for negative ones.** Here is a straightforward way to eliminate negative thoughts and not resist. What you resist persists. Hence, when a negative thought comes, please don't push it away. Acknowledge it. Then, substitute it with a thought about anything positive that has happened to you in the past. It can even be the same positive thought each time. For instance, I think about the scorching summer day when I was with my two kids at the

pool. And for some strange reason, we were the only people at the pool besides the lifeguards. The lifeguards allowed us to jump off the guard chair and do anything we wanted. It was a wonderful day. I can use that same thought anytime and as much as I choose.

I recommend having four to five positive past experiences that you can easily recall when negative thinking arises. Write down and reflect on five positive thoughts or experiences from your past. Store them in your memory or on your phone. The only rule is they must be positive. Let these become your go-to repertoire of positive thoughts you can recall in seconds to replace and thus distract from negative thoughts. This will help to at least slow the momentum of negative thoughts.

5. **Establish Specific and Tangible Goals for Positivity**. — no excuses, just action. Momentum and energy come from deliberate effort, so create daily, weekly, and monthly goals that anchor positivity. Start now:

- Daily: Give five genuine compliments to others and five to yourself. No exceptions. Build the habit of lifting yourself and those around you.

- Weekly: Perform three intentional acts of kindness for acquaintances and three for strangers. Kindness generates positivity and reinforces your mindset.

- Monthly: Commit to a concrete goal, like running five days a week until you can run five miles nonstop. While running, focus your thoughts only on positivity: "The weather is great," "I love this neighborhood," or even an imagined moment of happiness. Your thoughts don't need to be rooted in reality—they need to make you feel good.

6. **Surround yourself with positive people.** The company you keep directly shapes your outlook, decisions, and, ultimately, your life. Make it your top priority to spend time with people who inspire and support you and those who are actively growing and striving for greatness. Seek out mentors, sponsors, and friends who challenge you, push you toward your dreams, and offer constructive, actionable advice.

A true mentor doesn't just guide—they want to see you exceed their own success. A sponsor goes further, advocating for you, speaking your name in rooms where you're not present, and using their influence to open doors and create opportunities. These relationships are critical to your growth and success. The people you surround yourself with also determine your financial trajectory. As Jim Rohn famously said, "You are the average of the five people you spend the most time with." If your goals include greater achievements and income, align yourself with individuals who embody those outcomes.

Reaching out to mentors or sponsors may require persistence. They are busy for a reason—they've earned their success. Don't take it personally if they don't have time for you. Keep trying, and if one door closes, knock on another. Your determination will speak volumes.

Who you allow into your circle is your choice—and that choice will define your future. Choose wisely.

7. **Reading.** Reading is not optional—it is a powerful, required tool for personal growth and transformation. It develops and sharpens your mindset, introducing you to the latest ideas, cultures, and philosophies that broaden your perspective and make your outlook more flexible and adaptable. Immersing yourself in motivational, spiritual, or self-improvement books—or any genre that challenges and grows you—gives you the tools to evolve and succeed.

Reading doesn't just enrich your knowledge; it hones your problem-solving skills, forcing you to think critically about complex ideas and challenges. It equips you with fresh perspectives, making you sharper and more effective in tackling real-world problems.

The reflective nature of reading pushes you to introspect, identify areas for growth, and apply these lessons to your life. It's not just a passive activity; it's an active investment in your future, enriching your mindset and expanding the reservoir of knowledge you draw from when making decisions.

If you're serious about improving your life, reading is a discipline you cannot ignore. Pick up a book, dive in, and upgrade yourself—one page at a time.

8. **Experiences.** Be sure to continuously seek out new experiences, for they help profoundly shape your mindset. New and old adventures serve as real-world classrooms

where we access, adjust, and hone our beliefs, attitudes, and reactions about every aspect of our lives. These experiences, whether positive or challenging, are vital in developing resilience, adaptability, and capacity for growth.

Engaging with new situations pushes you to learn and evolve. Facing adversity teaches you resilience, helping you see setbacks as temporary hurdles rather than insurmountable obstacles. And overcoming challenges boosts your confidence and reinforces your belief in your ability to effect change in your life.

Thus, experiences are unequivocally necessary for shaping and changing your mindset and equipping you to navigate the expected difficulties of life with confidence and purpose.

You will have experiences every day, whether or not you consciously ask for them or seek them. You are responsible for turning every experience into one that serves your interests without causing harm to anyone. Hence, each night before you fall asleep, think about an experience you had during the day that did not serve you. Reflect on it, visualize and thus revise the event how you would have preferred it to play out. When your mindset is focused and clear, you will be better equipped to make fast, rational, and intelligent decisions.

Chapter Two:

Confidence Is a Skill You Can Build and Own

"With confidence, you have won before you have started."
– Marcus Garvey

Confidence is the ability to trust yourself and your capacity to accomplish a task. It is a skill that can be learned and strengthened. No matter where you are now, your confidence can and will improve with consistent effort.

Confidence doesn't appear overnight, but it will grow steadily based on your work. Consider the most disciplined professional basketball player of all time, Kobe Bryant. His confidence and skill increased because of his repetition and relentless dedication to mental and physical training. During the off-season, he started his days at 4 a.m. and worked out six hours a day, six days a week. Compare that to the average NBA player who trains just 11 hours a week during the same period. Kobe understood the power of repetition. The more you practice, the faster your skills improve and the more reliable they become.

To build your confidence, focus on consistent action. Start small. Pick one skill to work on and add more as you go. You don't need to perfect one area before moving on to the next. The keys are repetition and steady progress, not perfection.

"Perfect is the enemy of good" means that striving for perfection can prevent progress and impede completion. The pursuit of flawlessness can lead to procrastination, endless revisions, or even quitting tasks because nothing ever seems "good enough." This thinking can block achievement and prevent you from appreciating solid, successful outcomes.

Instead, focus on finishing. A good outcome that gets done is always better than an unfinished project held back by the pursuit of perfection. Aim high, but don't let the fear of imperfection stop you from moving forward. Confidence is built through action, and every step forward strengthens your belief in what you can accomplish.

To increase your confidence, ask yourself: **"Who am I, and Who do I want to become?"** Why start this way? Reflecting deeply on the person you want to be creates a north star for building true, lasting confidence. Knowing who you aim to become provides direction and clarity for your decisions, behaviors, and responses. Here's why this is crucial:

1. **Anchors Your Identity**
    2. A clear sense of who you are keeps you grounded. It makes you less susceptible to external opinions and helps build confidence that doesn't waver.

3. Simplifies Decisions

When your choices align with your values and vision, decision-making becomes straightforward. If a decision doesn't align with who you want to be, you don't consider it.

4. Builds Determination

A keen sense of self gives you the grit to push through setbacks. You stay committed to your goals, even when the path gets tough.

5. Reduces Self-Doubt

Knowing your identity silences second-guessing. It strengthens your confidence by affirming your choices and reinforcing your direction.

6. Attracts Opportunities

Confidence rooted in purpose attracts the right opportunities. People and situations that align with your vision will naturally come to you.

Here's something to consider: What is the number one quality leaders say is essential for success? Confidence. The best part is confidence is not something you're born with; it's something you build. You set the change in motion when you decide to strengthen your self-confidence. That choice is decisive and assertive and marks the beginning of something greater. Progress starts the instant you commit. All it takes is your commitment to the journey—to begin your single step.

Here are the five skills to help you increase your confidence:

1. **Self-talk** - This is the most important skill for increasing your confidence. The comments you say to yourself purposely *and* your habitual thoughts about yourself.

   ❖ **Habitual thoughts** – as discussed in Chapter 1, your habitual thoughts are what you are thinking when you are not consciously or intentionally thinking. For example, when you are alone, sitting in class, or a meeting, you are thinking are your habitual thoughts.

   Your thoughts should be encouraging and uplifting. It is your mind you get to say and create anything you want about yourself. What you consistently tell yourself is what your mind believes. Say great things to yourself like:

   a) "No one better" or "They're not like me": This is the absolute truth for everyone. There are seven billion people on this earth, and no one is exactly like you. There is no one better at being you.

   b) "All I do is win!": Every situation has two outcomes— you win, or you learn. A "loss" is a lesson, and lessons are wins.

   c) "I don't take losses, I learn lessons!" Adopt this mindset, and setbacks won't shake you.

   d) When doubts arise, don't ask, "Can I?" Ask, "Is there any way?" That shift unlocks potential.

2. **Appreciation – Build Confidence Through Daily Gratitude** -Learn the daily practice of appreciation. Be thankful for what others often overlook: waking up, having food, seeing, hearing, breathing. These are victories. There is good in every single day—find it, acknowledge it, and focus on it. Without exception, there is always something worth celebrating.

❖ **Celebrate Small Wins Every Day** - Identify and acknowledge at least five small wins daily. These wins can be as simple as waking up on time, completing a workout, or making progress on a task. Small victories are significant—they are the building blocks of long-term success.

❖ Appreciation shifts your focus from what is missing to what's working. It builds resilience and reinforces the belief that every effort counts. The more you celebrate your wins, the more confident and unstoppable you become. Make appreciation a daily habit—a powerful tool for achieving lasting growth and confidence.

3. **Boldly Protect Your Access, and Guard Your Mental Fortress -** not everyone or everything deserves access to you. Allowing the wrong influences inside weakens your confidence, clarity, and growth. Enforce these non-negotiable strategies to protect your mental space:

   i. **Ruthlessly Cut Your Circle in Half**

   Your circle directly shapes your future. Surround yourself with negativity, and you will become part of it. If nine people in your life are unmotivated or toxic, you will be the tenth. Period. On the other hand, aligning with nine positive, driven individuals elevates your mindset, actions, and trajectory. Be intentional about who stays in your life. If someone doesn't uplift, inspire, or support you, they do not benefit your circle.

ii. Slash Social Media Usage to Under One Hour Daily

Social media is one of the greatest drains on confidence and mental clarity. It fosters comparison, plants seeds of inadequacy, and distracts users from their goals. To break free from its toxic cycle, limit your usage to one hour per day.

Reclaim that time and redirect it toward actions that bring clarity, purpose, and momentum.

iii. Commit to Four Hours of Digital Silence Daily

Every day, dedicate at least four hours to complete disconnection—no texts, emails, calls, or distractions. One way to help with this is to turn off your phone. The constant barrage of digital noise steals your focus, disrupts your energy, and slows your progress. Four hours may be too much to do initially, so begin with one hour, then two hours, then more.

Boldly Guard Your Mind

Your mind is your most valuable asset—guard it fiercely. Control who and what gains access to it because not everyone deserves your time, and not everything deserves your attention. Monitor everything that seeks to influence you: the music you listen to, the podcasts you follow, the social media you consume, and the shows or movies you watch. Their primary goal is to occupy your mind. You must defend it with unwavering determination.

This is your life, your success, and your growth—protect them with bold, unapologetic boundaries. The world will always demand more from you, but your ability to succeed hinges on how well you guard your energy and focus. Treat your mind as a fortress. Guard it relentlessly, and you'll unlock clarity, confidence, and unstoppable momentum.

4. Dress the Part—Command Your Confidence and Presence

Your attire is more than just clothing; it is a tool that directly influences how you see yourself and how others perceive you. Before you can say a word, your dress must communicate competence, confidence, and authority. Wearing professional attire—whether a suit, coordinated clothing, or anything associated with power—triggers subconscious changes in your mindset and behavior. You stand taller, make stronger eye contact, and project assertiveness.

Dressing with purpose is a form of preparation, putting you in the right frame of mind to tackle challenges before you even begin. Dressing the part also pertains to how you dress in your environment. A clean and organized space eliminates distractions. Your environment must reflect order and purpose because it dictates your mindset and actions.

5. Preparation: The Non-Negotiable Foundation of Confidence

Preparation is the ultimate confidence booster. It eliminates uncertainty, silences anxiety, and puts you firmly in control. When you're prepared, you don't just feel ready—you are ready.

Preparation ensures peak performance under pressure and sharpens one's ability to handle setbacks with grit and composure. It strengthens one's mindset, replacing doubt with self-assurance and fueling positive self-talk. Preparation converts nervous energy into laser-focused motivation by anticipating challenges and controlling one's response.

Confidence isn't given—it's earned through preparation. Be relentless. Be ready. Be unstoppable.

6. Daily Dominate Your Environment—No Exceptions

Controlling your environment is non-negotiable for building confidence and achieving success. Your surroundings dictate your mindset and actions. Say no to distractions and unnecessary commitments without hesitation. What you say yes to or agree to makes you accountable.

❖ Strategically Plan Your Day

Spend ten minutes each morning writing down the schedule and plan for your day. Don't leave your time to chance or external demands. Take control of your schedule, and you take control of your results. Confidence thrives on consistent, intentional action.

Confidence is not a gift; it's a choice and a skill you can build. Every action you choose to take—every rep, every small win, every step outside your comfort zone—moves you closer to the person you're meant to be. Don't let fear, perfectionism, or negativity hold you back; they are no match for deliberate action and ruthless preparation. This is your time to rise. Define who you are, control your space, and attack daily with purpose. The world responds to confidence—claim yours, and there is nothing you can't achieve. This is your moment to seize control, push past limits, and claim- the confidence to elevate your life. You're not waiting for success—you're preparing to dominate it. Be unstoppable.

Chapter Three:

— ⟩⟩⟩ —

Types of Decisions

"The hardest thing to learn in life is which bridge to cross and which to burn."

David Russell

I t's helpful to recognize the spectrum of decision types we pass through daily. From the routine choices that shape our mornings to the strategic deliberations that chart our future, each decision type plays a crucial role in our personal and professional lives. Having a rudimentary understanding of the distinct types of decisions and learning how to make fast decisions efficiently will improve your decision-making ability.

This book will move you quickly to being a fast decision expert. To that end, it is important to have a working understanding of several types of decisions. Think of it like being a medical student who wants to be an emergency medicine physician. While they know what specialty they want to enter, the student should still rotate through the core specialties (pediatrics, internal medicine, psychiatry, surgery, and OB/GYN) so that they have a rudimentary understanding of the full range of medical care. This will benefit them from the different specialties intercept and the range of care offered. Similarly, there are various ranges and intersections of several types of decisions.

Let's briefly discuss the six most common types of decisions.

1. **Routine Decisions** are daily automatic decisions that require little thought or effort: what color socks to wear, whether to have cereal or eggs for breakfast and which movie to see. Most of our daily decisions are inconsequential and have no significant impact.

2. **Slow Decisions.** These are choices that are made over a more extended period. They often require extensive deliberation, analysis, and research. Slow decisions include:

   ❖ **Strategic Decisions** involve long-term planning and outcome-setting, such as where to buy a house, where to send your kids to school, and when to launch a new product line or enter a new market.

   ❖ **Operational Decisions** are the choices you make daily to ensure smooth operation, optimize efficiency, and achieve short-term objectives. Examples include planning your family's daily schedule to balance household chores and homework, scheduling maintenance services for the house or cars, and, in business, inventory management, customer service, or scheduling.

❖ **Problem-solving decisions.** These require critical thinking, analysis of information, obtaining additional information, and often including family members, team members, or other stakeholders in the decision process. Examples:

- Troubleshooting a malfunctioning household appliance, such as a refrigerator. You might diagnose the problem by checking for common issues like power supply or temperature settings. Then, decide whether to attempt a do-it-yourself repair or call a professional technician.

- In business, resolving a customer complaint about an expired product. The customer service team would investigate the issue, gather relevant information about the complaint, and decide on the best course of action to satisfy the customer, such as offering to replace the old product with a new one, issuing a refund, or providing support to address the customer's problem with the product.

3. **Fast Decisions.** These are choices that are made without extensive deliberation or lengthy analysis. Fast decisions rely on expertise, intuition, past experiences, and instinctual judgment. Often, the information available at the time is not optimal. I'll give more detailed examples here since this is the subject of the book:

❖ **Medical.** One late spring day in the ER, I encountered a patient presenting with symptoms that suggested severe conditions. He was an 18-year-old student—I'll call him Jack. He'd spent time with his class at a park across the street from a hospital. During their lunch break, Jack took a sip from his soda can and set it aside to chat with his friends. Moments later, he suddenly felt a sharp sting in his mouth when he went for another sip. When he looked down, he discovered a bee leaving the soda can.

The schoolteacher immediately took him to the emergency room, which, fortunately, was across the street. When I examined Jack, he was initially in good spirits, talking and joking with his friends, who had come to the ER with him. The teacher had contacted Jack's mother, who was also at his bedside. He showed no signs of distress. However, during the physical examination, Jack said, "My tongue feels funny." This signaled that his tongue could be swelling as an allergic or inflammatory response from the bee sting. When this happens because of a bug sting, airway obstruction can occur rapidly.

Faced with a crucial decision, I weighed my options: first, administer IV medications like diphenhydramine, steroids, and possibly epinephrine, which are standard treatments for allergic reactions but can take up to 15 minutes to become effective. Or intubate—this is an emergency procedure where a flexible tube is inserted through the mouth into the trachea (windpipe) to maintain an open airway and assist with breathing—a procedure in which there is a small risk of not being able to place the tube correctly in the airway, in which case the patient will suffocate to death.

Jack's airway was closing quickly because of the rapid swelling caused by the bee sting. So, I opted for immediate intubation. Just as I was preparing for the procedure, Jack's speech became muffled, and he started to drool – another ominous sign that his throat was beginning to close. I started the intubation, but the airway was already so swollen that I could not see the trachea. His oxygen saturation started to fall because he was not breathing. To make matters more stressful, we had allowed his mother to stay in the room during the procedure. I had a young 18-year-old healthy male who could no longer breathe on his own, and his mother was sitting right next to him, holding his hand.

I quickly repositioned his head and neck. I was able to see the windpipe and place the tube successfully. The oxygen saturation never dropped below 94 percent, meaning his brain never went without oxygen. I heavily sedated Jack and transferred him to the ICU for close monitoring. A few days later, he was discharged in excellent health, a relief to everyone involved.

❖ **Business.** With four days until the launch of seven new products at the vitamin and supplement company where you're a manager, you're hit with a curveball: Sha', the team member overseeing the launch, is suddenly out due to the flu. There's no time for hesitation or lengthy strategy sessions. Relying on your experience in handling demanding situations and understanding each team member's strengths, you make a swift decision. You assign Gerald, a new team member with previous launch experience, as the team lead, even though you haven't seen him in action yet. You redistribute the workload, giving Gerald the critical tasks and assigning smaller tasks to others based on their skills, ensuring efficiency and maintaining team morale and energy levels. These quick decisions keep your project on track and highlight your trust in your team's capabilities and ability to navigate challenges with confidence and clarity. It's a clear demonstration of leadership: making prompt, informed decisions to keep things running smoothly, even when faced with unexpected obstacles.

4. **Split-second Decisions.** These decisions are made when there is extremely limited time- usually seconds, and a lack of information, and the consequences are critical. Examples:

❖ **Personal:** You have boarded a flight that is already running late. The airline announces that you will miss your connecting flight just before closing the door. This means you would be stuck in the airport for four hours, thus arriving at least an hour late for your seven-year-old daughter's first piano recital, which you promised to attend. Your alternative is to rent a car and drive eight hours, ensuring you arrive exactly on time, assuming no delays. Do you get off the flight before they close the door, or do you stay on board?

❖ **Business:** Your company's server may have been compromised. You notice unusual account activity, anomalies in network traffic, and suspicious files and changes, leading you to realize that you have been hacked. It will take a few hours to determine the source of the breach—whether it's from a trojan, a subcontractor, or internal espionage. Given that your entire business model relies on online orders, you face a critical decision: do you close part of the server to stop new orders and prevent further data theft, or do you let the server continue functioning?

5. **Tactical Decisions**. There is often plenty of time for these, but not as much as for slow decisions. Tactical decisions are made to achieve specific objectives within a limited timeframe. These decisions focus on the short- to medium-term actions and initiatives that contribute to the overall strategic goals of the person, household, or business. Tactical decisions involve planning and executing actions to address predictable or immediate challenges. These decisions are oriented towards managing daily tasks, overcoming obstacles, and progressing towards long-term aspirations. Examples:

❖ **Personal.** Suppose you have a crucial job interview early in the morning in a bustling city. A smart move would be to review your interview notes and choose what you will wear the evening before. Plan to head out an hour earlier than you think you need to, just in case you hit unexpected traffic. These short-term decisions are tactical because they help you achieve the long-term goal of securing the job you desire.

❖ **Business.** Tactical decisions are the operational choices managers and teams make to execute strategic plans effectively. They include allocating resources, deploying personnel, and implementing processes to achieve predefined objectives within a given timeframe. Tactical decisions bridge the gap between day-to-day operations and strategic goals, guiding the organization toward its desired outcomes. A good example would be Shieldvitamins.com's decision in 2023 to discount its entire current inventory to make room for new products.

A final crucial point is that fatigue can significantly impair your decision-making ability in various areas. Avoid making important decisions when you're exhausted, as your fatigue will impact your judgment. In Chapter Five, we'll discuss techniques for steadying your nerves.

Chapter Four:

—⁓—

Neuroplasticity and Decision-making

"The measure of intelligence is the ability to change."

-Albert Einstein

The pathways the brain uses for decision-making are not linear. While the intricate anatomical structures involved in decision-making are beyond the scope of this discussion, one key concept is vital to understand: the brain is composed of specialized cells called neurons. These neurons process and transmit electrical and chemical signals, enabling communication between different areas of the brain and throughout the body. They serve as the fundamental building blocks of the nervous system.

The human brain and nervous system contain an astonishing 90 billion neurons, each interconnected to form complex networks. These networks are not static; they significantly shape how we think, learn, and make decisions. Neuroplasticity is a crucial term for decision-making, often called brain plasticity or neural plasticity. Neuroplasticity is the brain's remarkable ability to adapt and reorganize itself in response to new experiences, learning, or environmental changes. But your brain is not fixed—

it is dynamic and capable of evolving throughout your life. This capacity for change allows the brain to physically alter its structure, connections, and functions based on your experience. More profoundly, this means you can actively reshape your brain through intentional effort.

Consider how this concept is utilized in individuals recovering from a cerebral vascular accident, also known as a stroke. A stroke can damage parts of the brain, often leading to impairments in movement, speech, or cognitive functions. Yet, through consistent rehabilitation exercises and therapies, the brain can create new neuronal pathways to compensate for the damaged areas. This process enables many stroke survivors to regain functionality and improve their quality of life.

Take the story of John, a stroke patient. After his stroke, the right side of John's brain sustained damage, significantly affecting motor functions on the left side of his body. This caused weakness in his left arm and leg, challenging simple tasks and decisions challenging.

Through months of dedicated therapy and persistent effort, John's condition improved dramatically. He engaged his affected limbs in repetitive exercises and diverse therapies designed to stimulate new neural connections. Over time, his brain adapted by forming alternative pathways to bypass the damaged areas. John's progress is a powerful example of neuroplasticity in action, demonstrating the brain's ability to repair and reorganize itself.

John's journey underscores an important truth: the principles of neuroplasticity are not limited to stroke recovery. They are available to everyone. You can use neuroplasticity to train your brain to achieve anything, including improving decision-making. With purposeful focus and repetitive practice, you can create new neural pathways that enhance your ability to make quick and effective decisions. You can rewire your brain to better support your goals and aspirations by intentionally engaging it.

Neuroplasticity is a testament to the brain's flexibility and adaptability, reminding us that change is always possible—whether recovering from an injury or mastering a new skill.

Here is a sports-focused example of neuroplasticity in action. Tom, a high school basketball player eager to improve his free throw accuracy. After a less-than-stellar season in terms of free throw accuracy, Tom, guided by his coach, realized his shooting form needed refinement for better consistency.

Neuroplastic Process:

1. **Detailed Review and Feedback:** Tom started by analyzing video footage of his shooting technique with his coach. They pinpointed specific parts of his form—like his grip, alignment, and follow-through—that needed improvement.

2. **Focused Repetition:** He dedicated much time each day to practicing his free throws, emphasizing the corrections identified. Repeating the right movements hundreds of times was crucial to embedding these skills in his muscle memory.

3. **Step-by-Step Adjustments:** Over several weeks, Tom and his coach addressed one adjustment at a time, allowing him to focus on mastering each movement thoroughly without feeling overwhelmed.

4. **Visualization:** In addition to physical practice, Tom engaged in mental visualization. He would imagine executing flawless free throws, focusing on the tactile feel of the ball, his bodily movements, and seeing the ball go through the hoop.

Neuroplasticity at Work:

❖ **Strengthening Connections:** Each physical and mental rehearsal strengthened the connections in Tom's brain related to his shooting technique. This synaptic strengthening made the necessary movements more automatic and efficient.

❖ **Brain Adaptation:** As Tom improved, the motor control areas of his brain, which were responsible for coordinating his shooting motion, adapted.

Months of diligent practice paid off. Tom's free throw accuracy improved fifty-one percent by the end of the season, and his refined technique became instinctual.

Tom's journey demonstrates how applying neuroplasticity through practice and mental strategies can lead to tangible improvements. By continuously engaging his body and mind, Tom made lasting changes in his brain, translating into improved athletic performance. He intentionally created new pathways. The brain's capacity to form new pathways and connections enhances decision-making speed. In other words, you can improve your ability to make quick decisions via practice.

The following is a detailed process. The simple concept is you can change the anatomy of your brain to make it function the way you have intentionally trained it. To improve fast decision-making through neuroplasticity, consider the following example:

*Scenario: You are a professional working on quick decision-making in high-pressure situations. Imagine you are an executive, manager, or leader who regularly faces high-pressure, fast-paced situations where quick decisions are crucial. In this example, you will be a manager.

You can utilize neuroplasticity by adopting a structured approach:

1. **Cognitive Drills and Simulations**

   The manager practices decision-making under simulated stress conditions, such as role-playing scenarios in which rapid calls must be made within a limited time frame. Timed decision-making exercises mimic real-life situations, creating neural pathways that make quick thinking more natural. This needs to be done repetitively.

   ❖ For instance, the manager is given a scenario in which a customer complains loudly about a missing item, another employee asks for guidance on an urgent issue, and a technical problem shuts down the checkout system.

   ❖ The manager must decide how to prioritize and address each situation within three minutes, considering customer satisfaction, team morale, and operational efficiency.

2. Reflection and Review

After each simulation, the manager reviews their performance, noting which decisions were effective and which could improve. This feedback loop helps the brain learn from mistakes and adapt, reinforcing beneficial decision-making patterns.

3. Mindfulness and Focus Training

Incorporating daily mindfulness practices helps the manager improve their focus and stay calm under pressure. This training reduces reactivity in high-stakes situations and supports clearer thinking, enhancing their ability to make rapid decisions without emotional interference. *(See Chapter Three for more information on mindfulness.)*

4. Physical Activity for Brain Health

The manager regularly engages in regular aerobic exercises, such as running or cycling, to boost blood flow and stimulate growth factors that enhance brain function. Physical fitness improves overall cognitive speed, making fast decision-making more efficient.

5. Learning from Diverse Experiences

Managers deliberately place themselves in unfamiliar situations to build adaptability, such as learning a new skill or taking on tasks outside their comfort zone. This trains the brain to be more flexible and better equipped to process unexpected challenges quickly.

6. **Simulation Games and Complex Puzzles**

They spend time on strategic games that require quick thinking, like chess with a timer or fast-paced video games. These activities require making split-second choices and adapting strategies on the fly, strengthening neural circuits associated with rapid decision-making.

Over time, these repetitive, timed simulations help the manager build neural pathways for assessing priorities, staying calm under pressure, and making effective decisions quickly. This "muscle memory" for decision-making becomes more natural during real-life stressful situations.

By practicing these targeted strategies regularly, the manager enhances their brain's neuroplasticity, leading to better, faster decision-making in real-life high-pressure scenarios.

The following scenario shows how to use neuroplasticity to help with fast decisions.

*Scenario: A Corporate Manager Dealing with a Major Crisis

A corporate manager leads a team through unexpected crises, such as sudden financial downturns, major client issues, or internal system failures. Quick, strategic decision-making is essential to mitigate risks and keep the business running smoothly. Here is how they can use the TIC-D framework to improve their decision-making skills:

1. **Time – Training to Make Quick Decisions Under Pressure**

   The manager practices making decisions within strict time limits during crisis simulation exercises. These drills help train their brain to assess situations and act within limited timeframes, building the mental agility needed for real crises.

   Example: The manager participates in role-playing crisis simulations where they must decide on an action plan within 15 minutes. This repeated practice strengthens the neural pathways for fast decision-making under pressure.

2. **Information – Focusing on Critical Data**

   The manager practices gathering and filtering only essential information needed to make informed decisions. This helps prevent information overload and ensures they act based on relevant data when under pressure.

   For example, a manager might simulate quick briefing sessions with their team, during which they have only five minutes to review key data points related to the crisis. This practice helps reinforce the brain's ability to identify and prioritize critical information quickly.

3. **Critical Consequences – Weighing Potential Outcomes Swiftly**

The manager practices evaluating the consequences of various choices quickly. They learn to balance potential risks and benefits, ensuring their decision supports the company's best interests.

Example: The manager runs through scenario drills where they assess the impact of potential strategies (e.g., halting production to address a quality issue or continuing at risk). Regularly practicing these assessments helps build the brain's capacity for rapid consequence evaluation.

4. **Committing to Decisions with Confidence**

The manager practices making final decisions and sticking with them confidently, even under pressure. Then, they reflect on these choices post-simulation to understand what worked well and where adjustments are needed. This feedback loop reinforces learning and strengthens the brain's adaptability.

Example: The manager conducts drills where they must decide (e.g., issuing a public statement or changing a project's course) and commits to it within a set time limit. Post-drill reviews help solidify their learning and improve future decision-making.

Result: By applying the TIC-D framework in training and real-life situations, the manager builds neuroplasticity, strengthening their ability to make fast, strategic decisions. This ongoing practice ensures they can act decisively, confidently, and effectively in high-pressure situations, benefiting the company and the team they lead.

Now, you may be wondering what this TIC-D method is that is mentioned in the above scenario. The **TIC-D Method,** otherwise known as Time, Information, Critical Consequences, and Decision, is a process I created to assist in making fast and critical decisions under pressure. But it is more than a checklist for making decisions; it is a deliberate system that leverages the power of **neuroplasticity**—your brain's ability to rewire itself through practice.

Every time you work through **Time, Information, Critical Consequences, and Decisions**, you are doing four crucial things for your brain:

❖ **Repetition Strengthens Neural Pathways:** Each time you practice making fast decisions with the TIC-D structure, you strengthen the specific neural circuits responsible for assessing a situation quickly, identifying relevant information, evaluating outcomes, and committing to a decision. This repetition is the foundation of neuroplasticity.

❖ **Creating Mental Shortcuts (Automaticity):** As you repeatedly apply the TIC-D method, your brain automates parts of the process. Instead of consciously working through each step slowly, your brain starts recognizing patterns and firing those pathways faster. Over time, what once required effort becomes second nature—leading to **faster, more confident decisions**.

❖ **Reducing Cognitive Load:** Regularly training your brain under pressure (simulations, timed drills) reduces the mental energy required for high-stakes decisions. Neuroplasticity allows your brain to **optimize** the pathways involved, making decisions more intuitive and less exhausting.

❖ **Bridging to Real-Life Scenarios:** Practicing TIC-D in simulations mimics the stress and complexity of real-life crises. When a real situation hits, your brain recognizes the pattern and **accesses the trained pathway**, enabling you to respond quickly and accurately.

This is the power of neuroplasticity: Every time you engage with the TIC-D method, you are not just improving your decision-making skills—you are physically rewiring your brain to be faster, sharper, and more resilient when it matters most. *(We will dive deeper into the TIC-D method and its practices in Chapter Seven.)*

Chapter Five:

—⤳—

Steady Your Nerves

"Such a man needs not courage but nerve control and cool-headedness. This he can get only by daily practice."
-Theodore Roosevelt

One of the most striking examples of steady nerves is found in Mahatma Gandhi's life. His relentless nonviolent resistance to British rule in India continues to be a testament to inner calm's power. Consider the Salt March of 1930. This wasn't just a protest but a 240-mile march against the oppressive British salt tax. Throughout this grueling journey, Gandhi and his followers faced relentless challenges—physical exhaustion, threats of violence, and the looming threat of arrest. Yet Gandhi remained unshaken, and his calm was a direct result of his meditation and spiritual discipline. His nerves of steel were on full display as he inspired thousands to join him, maintaining a peaceful and disciplined movement against all odds. When Gandhi finally reached the coastal town of Dandi, he made a simple yet powerful gesture: he bent down and picked up a lump of salt, defying British law with a quiet but profound act of rebellion. This single act, executed with unwavering composure, electrified the Indian independence movement and drew the eyes of the world to their cause.

Even when the British authorities arrested him shortly after, Gandhi's calm did not waver. His unflinching advocacy for nonviolence and peace continued unabated. Gandhi's steady nerves, honed through years of meditation, were not just crucial—they were the bedrock of his leadership and the driving force behind India's path to independence.

Steadying your nerves means owning your calm. Simply put, it means controlling your composure and emotions in stressful situations. Stay focused, and do not let fear, anxiety, or excitement knock you off course. This is your call to action for those critical moments when you must think clearly and act boldly and decisively.

Controlling your nerves is essential, especially when the stakes are sky-high and every decision matters. Unsteady nerves can sneak up on you, often at critical times. Think of your mental strength as muscle training—just as you hit the gym to build strong muscles, you must consistently strengthen your mental fortitude.

The key difference between strength of mind and emotional grit training is that it happens in silence, away from the eyes of others. It's a battle fought in the quiet of your mind, sometimes in the dark. This is where you push yourself, challenge your limits, and never back down. During these quiet moments, your effort will reveal itself when the spotlight is on. What you do in the dark will shine through the light.

Embrace this process, turn your nerves into your greatest weapon, and face this ongoing battle with relentless intensity and unwavering determination. Continuously improve and optimize your mental resilience, and you'll become unstoppable. Learning to steady your nerves is a marathon, not a sprint. In other words, it may take longer than you would like but consistently stick to the process. "Those who do not quit will be winners." Win!

Four activities to improve mental toughness:

1. **Mindful Meditation**

   Mindful meditation is a practice that involves focusing on the present moment with full awareness, without judgment or negative emotion. It is an acceptance of whatever is happening to you right then during your intentional meditation. It helps reduce stress and improve emotional well-being by promoting a non-judgmental and accepting attitude toward one's thoughts and feelings. What others have said or tried to make you feel is none of your business. Only your thoughts and feelings matter. You connect to your natural inner voice, which is always tied to your inner strength. And yes, we all have natural inner strength. The natural calm in the morning is the ideal time for mindful meditation. This is how to do it:

   i. Go to a quiet room where you will not be disturbed. No cell phone, no music. No sounds.

   ii. Find a comfortable position, either sitting up or lying flat.

iii. Set a time limit. It is best to start with two to three minutes. When building a habit, you must start simple and then build on it. You can then build to 30 minutes or more.

iv. Quiet your mind by thinking about something positive and straightforward that makes you feel good.

v. Close your eyes, inhale deeply, and then slowly exhale for ten seconds. Focus only on the sensations of your breath in your body. Do this five times. If you notice your mind wandering away from the sensations of your breath, gently bring it back.

vi. Expand your awareness. In addition to your breathing, try listening to your heartbeat and noticing sounds in your environment. First, notice sounds in the room where you're meditating, then any sounds you hear regardless of location. If you are outside, listen to a leaf falling or the wind moving the trees. Keep your breaths gentle and slow.

viii. After a few days to a week of practicing this exercise, you will notice changes in your thought patterns. They will be clearer, helping you to make better decisions in life and faster decisions under pressure. You may find that answers to questions or problems come to you during meditation. If they do, make a mental note of them and write them down when the meditation concludes. Regular meditation increases resilience, calmness, and mental clarity.

2. **Physical Activity**

❖ Your mind and body are one. You must do the same with your body as you train and strengthen your mind. The American Heart Association recommends 150 minutes of physical activity per week. You can and should do more. There are 168 hours in a week. You should commit to at least five hours per week of exercise. The threshold is that your activity or activities must make you sweat.

3. **Thoughts**

❖ Reframe your thoughts, turning fear-inducing *what-if*s into empowering narratives that propel you towards dreaming big. Actively challenge and change negative thoughts that contribute to fear. Flip the script on those fear-based thoughts! Swap "What if I fail?" with "What if I conquer?" or "What epic tale will this experience be a part of?" This mindset makeover shifts you from dread to dream and expect big.

Re-framing example:

❖ **Negative**: "I always mess up."

❖ **Challenge**: "What about my successes?"

❖ **Reframe**: "I make mistakes but learn and succeed too."

❖ **Affirmation**: "I am capable of improving every day."

Repeating several self-affirming mantras to yourself in silence several times daily is important. What you say to yourself regularly becomes real. It becomes who you are. Your words help shape your self-image, which becomes the beacon for how you move through the world.

A mantra is a word or phrase you repeat to yourself to help instill a mindset or set of helpful beliefs. It's a tool for mental clarity and motivation, often used in meditation or daily life.

Here are a few examples:

"I am strong."

"I am more than enough."

"Let it go, keep moving."

"I will be kind and strong."

Practice regularly to shift your mindset from negative to positive.

4. **The Art of Visualization or Mental Moviemaking:**

Mental Moviemaking is where you are the hero, and things end as you want them to. The art of mental movie-making allows you to visualize success in vivid detail, training your brain for real-life bravery. Through this, you will:

❖ Improve your visualization skills by creating vivid, sensory-rich mental movies where you're the hero facing down fears and making bold decisions. It's not just about imagining but also incorporating feelings, sounds, or smells related to the event. Feel the victory, hear the applause, and smell the success. This is your brain's training ground for real-life bravery. You have complete control of the movie script, scenery, and outcome.

❖ Muhammad Ali is known worldwide as one of the greatest boxers of all time. Ali was a three-time heavyweight champion and Olympic gold medalist. He was revered not only for his dominance in the ring but also for his charisma, confidence, and work ethic. He also used visualization as a key strategy for maximum performance in the ring. Here is how Muhammad Ali approached it:

➢ Mental Practice: Ali mentally rehearsed his fights, vividly imagining every aspect of the bout before stepping into the ring. He visualized himself entering the arena, moving with agility, and flawlessly executing his boxing techniques.

➢ Environment: Ali would smell the arena like he was there. He would feel and picture the roar of the crowd.

➢ Tactical Planning: Beyond merely envisioning triumph, Ali used visualization to strategize his approach to each fight. He mentally sparred with opponents, anticipating their moves and devising counterattacks, giving himself a psychological advantage.

➢ Overcoming Challenges: Besides visualizing success, Ali imagined scenarios where he encountered adversity during a fight. He was mentally prepared to persevere through setbacks, bolstering his resilience and determination.

➢ Enhancing Focus: Visualization sharpened Ali's focus and concentration, enabling him to remain fully engaged in training and competition. He stayed motivated and committed to success by picturing himself achieving his goals.

➢ Muhammad Ali's incorporation of visualization into his training regimen was pivotal in his boxing career. It honed his physical skills and fortified his mental strength, underscoring his unwavering belief in his ability to triumph over any challenge in the ring.

You may ask, "What does building mental fortitude have to do with fast decision-making?" Everything! It's about developing a mindset of self-belief. You can't predict all the crucial fast decisions you'll face in life, but you know you'll be the one making them. Your confidence in yourself is paramount. The more time you spend on exercises and activities that boost your self-belief, the more your confidence grows.

You may say, "But visualization isn't real." It is confirmed in your mind. Visualization creates mental pathways that lead to actual changes in your brain. When you visualize yourself as the hero, your brain and mind become wired to be that hero. Have you ever seen a hero without confidence?

It is crucial to visualize your victory or success. Commit to practicing visualizing desired outcomes mentally three to four times a day. This discipline will significantly boost your confidence. For specific situations, meticulously envision your tactics and strategies. Anticipate potential challenges and mentally rehearse your responses. For example, if you're preparing for a significant speaking engagement, plan how you'll handle unexpected issues, like the microphone failing. Most importantly, you should always see yourself achieving your desired goal. This mental preparation will empower you to face any situation confidently and resiliently.

The Fast Decision Drills

The following are drills that will help you practice making fast decisions. Repetition is key. Some parts will resonate more than others for you. The goal is to make the drills your own so it serves you maximally and in the most poignant way. Let's get to work with some drills!

Here are a few rules:

- ❖ No one is always right, so don't expect to be.

- ❖ The goal is to make the first decision as soon as possible. The faster, the better. Why? You still have time to adjust if that first decision doesn't deliver the expected results. Every decision gets you to the next decision.

Challenge yourself with fast decision-making drills that simulate the need to think fast and make quick decisions. This could involve simulation games, sports, or role-playing exercises in personal or professional settings designed to replicate the pressures of fast decision-making in a safe environment. Like any other skill, decision-making improves with practice.

I'll give you three sample drills below. The first drill will require you to make small decisions in low-risk areas. The stakes of the second exercise will increase your tolerance for uncertainty. Finally, the third, higher-stakes drill will be the most challenging—it won't be about moving faster; it will be about facing a series of fast decisions, figuring out the most effective order in which to make those decisions, and executing.

Drill #1 - The 10-Minute Outfit Challenge:

1. **Set a Goal:** Decide on an activity or event you'll be dressing for, such as a casual outing, a work meeting, or an evening gathering.

2. **Set a Timer:** Give yourself exactly 10 minutes to choose a complete outfit, including accessories and shoes. Start the timer as soon as you open your closet.

3. **No Changes Allowed:** You're committed to the outfit once the timer is up. No swaps or additions.

4. **Reflect on Your Choice:** Evaluate how you felt about the outfit after the event. Did it match the occasion? Were you comfortable? If it fell short, what could you do differently next time?

5. **Optional Variation:** For added complexity, pick an outfit while considering specific constraints, such as needing layers for changing weather or selecting a professional outfit that's still comfortable for long hours.

This exercise helps you build confidence in your decision-making under time pressure by forcing you to make quick judgments without second-guessing. Over time, it trains you to prioritize essentials and trust your initial choices, even if they aren't perfect.

Drill #2 - Gym:

Remember the grocery store drill from the introduction to this book? You will use a similar format but apply it to working out at the gym. In other words, the drill is to give yourself less time than usual to do all the same exercises that you usually do. I suggest a 10% reduction in the time to start. But with fast decisions, you could complete the entire workout. You must adjust for when someone else is on the equipment and other factors that are beyond your control.

The time begins when you walk into the gym and includes changing into your gym clothes. And the time ends when you walk out of the gym door and includes showering/changing back into your street clothes.

Drill #3 – High Stakes

This drill is designed to prepare you for real-life health crises, improving your ability to stay calm, assess the situation, and make fast decisions that can have life-altering consequences.

Scenario: You are at home or in a public place, and someone suddenly collapses or experiences a serious medical emergency (e.g., a heart attack, stroke, choking, or severe bleeding). You have no immediate access to medical professionals, and your decisions in the next **5 minutes** could save the person's life.

Instructions:

1. The following background information is needed for the drill:

    ❖ **<u>Heart attack signs</u>** - chest pain or discomfort (often feeling like pressure or squeezing), shortness of breath, and pain radiating to the arms, neck, jaw, or back. Additional symptoms may include nausea, lightheadedness, and sweating.

    ❖ **<u>Stroke signs – FAST</u>** – is an acronym that helps recognize the signs of a stroke.

    > ➢ F: Face – is one side of the face drooping?

    > ➢ A: Arms – Can the person raise both arms or are they weak or numb?

    > ➢ S: Speech – slurred or strange speech?

    > ➢ T: Time – Call 911 immediately if any of these signs are present.

    ❖ <u>Choking signs</u> - the person may not be able to speak, cough, or breathe, and they may clutch their throat, turn blue, or exhibit panic. In severe cases, they may lose consciousness if the airway is not cleared.

    ❖ <u>Severe bleeding</u> - apply very firm and constant pressure to the wound with a clean cloth or bandage to help stop the blood flow and elevate the injured area if possible. Call emergency services immediately while continuing to apply pressure until help arrives.

2. **Set the Scenario**: Visualize or role-play a realistic health emergency. It could be any of the medical emergencies explained above or any urgent medical condition requiring immediate action. You can even have a friend or family member act out the scenario for realism.

  ❖ **Assess the Situation Quickly**: You only have **30 seconds** to assess what's going on. What are the person's symptoms? Are they breathing? Is their airway blocked? Is their heart beating? You must quickly decide if this is a heart-related emergency, choking, or something else requiring immediate first aid.

  ❖ **Decide on Immediate Actions**:

    1. **Heart Attack/Unconsciousness**: Begin CPR immediately if you determine that the person is not breathing and has no pulse.

    2. **Choking**: Administer the Heimlich maneuver if the airway is blocked.

    3. **Severe Bleeding**: Apply pressure to the wound or use a tourniquet if necessary to stop excessive bleeding.

  ❖ **Call for Help**: While performing first aid, call 911 or have someone nearby contact emergency services. If you're alone, decide when to stop rendering aid to make the call yourself.

❖ **Stay Calm and Reassess**: Continue providing aid while you wait for emergency services. If the person's condition changes (e.g., they regain consciousness or stop breathing again), make quick adjustments. Don't get stuck in one mindset—be prepared to switch from one action to another as the situation evolves.

❖ **Post-Scenario Reflection**: Once the drill is complete, evaluate your decisions. Did you recognize the correct symptoms? Did you act quickly enough? What went well, and where could you have improved your response?

This high-stakes drill prepares you for real-life medical emergencies, where fast, well-informed decisions can distinguish between life and death. It builds your confidence in responding to health-related crises and ensures you're better prepared for situations where quick action is essential.

Create Your Own Drills

Now, create your own low-, medium-, and high-stakes fast decision drills. Bear in mind that the high-stakes drill *is* a drill and should not carry serious life-impacting consequences. But do treat the drills like they are real life. Most importantly, the clock will be the main judge. Did you complete your drills within the determined time frame?

In these drills, as in life, lean into "failure" as a learning opportunity. I put "failure" in quotes because I believe there is no such thing as failure—only lessons. So, use these drills as practice in shifting your perspective on "failure." Instead of fearing it, see it as a valuable chance to learn. Every decision, whether successful or not, provides insights and lessons that can guide your future choices.

Steadying your nerves is key to being able to control the controllable. Focusing your energy on what's within your control requires mastering your emotions, which are the first thing you can control. Don't waste time on things outside your influence. For example, if you're organizing a groundbreaking ceremony with CEOs and politicians, and it starts to rain, don't wish for better weather—it's beyond your control. Instead, focus on moving the event indoors. By quickly identifying and accepting what you can't control, you'll reduce fear and anxiety, allowing you to fully focus on controlling the controllable.

As an ER doctor, I regularly undergo training designed to help me steady my nerves in high-pressure situations. Over time, this ability becomes ingrained in your mindset. You learn to remain calm in the face of chaos, and this skill extends beyond just medical emergencies to other challenging moments as well.

One particular incident involved an intoxicated patient who got off his stretcher and began causing a disturbance. As the attending physician, I approached him and calmly asked him to return to his stretcher, but he refused. I lowered the guardrails and repeated my request for him to get back in bed. Without warning, he grabbed me under the shoulder and tried to push me into a nearby single-person bathroom with a lock, all while threatening to harm me.

In that critical moment, I knew that steadying my nerves was crucial. Panic would have given him the advantage, allowing him to overpower me and close the door. Instead, I maintained my composure, dropped straight to the ground, causing him to trip. This quick action, born from remaining calm under pressure, caused enough commotion for the staff and security to intervene and restrain him. After sobering up, the patient was released without further incident. This situation highlighted the importance of practicing being able to control my nerves. When you remain calm and mentally strong, you can effectively manage the elements within your control, no matter how unpredictable or intense the situation.

The key is to decide fast, especially when information is limited. Fast decision-making, like any skill, requires practice. As the saying goes, "You don't wait until the storm to build a shelter." In the same way, don't wait for sudden, high-stakes decisions to begin improving this skill. Start practicing now for the crucial decisions you know lie ahead.

William Ernest Henley's poem "Invictus" exemplifies steady nerves:

Out of the night that covers me,
Black as the pit from pole to pole,
I thank whatever gods may be
For my unconquerable soul.

In the fell clutch of circumstance
I have not winced nor cried aloud.
Under the bludgeoning of chance
My head is bloody but unbowed.

Beyond this place of wrath and tears
Looms but the Horror of the shade,
And yet, the menace of the years
Finds and shall find me unafraid.

It matters not how strait the gate,
How charged with punishments the scroll,
I am the master of my fate,
I am the captain of my soul.

Chapter Six:

———⤳———

Fast Decision Habits

"In a moment of decision, the best thing you can do is the right thing, the next best thing is the wrong thing, and the worst thing you can do is nothing." - Theodore Roosevelt

Fast and optimal decision-making is built on small daily habits. You can achieve remarkable results over time through the disciplined repetition of minor improvements. This requires a structured framework—a guiding force that directs your focus and energy, preventing useless efforts and wasted potential. A framework provides guardrails without which you risk scattering your efforts and diluting your impact.

Consider the dedication of elite athletes: they don't aimlessly practice with the vague goal of greatness. Instead, they stick to rigorous routines that include diet, physical conditioning, skill drills, and mental preparation. This structured approach ensures their progress and excellence. Similarly, by establishing and internalizing your decision framework, you increase your ability to make swift, effective choices. Mastering decision-making lies in relentless practice and unwavering commitment to a well-defined process. Train your mind regularly, and through repetition, you will improve or develop the capacity for fast, confident decisions that lead to outstanding outcomes.

Below, I'll share some important habits that will help you stay on the path of clarity:

1. Expect to be right

Because mindset is so important to making successful fast decisions, I'm returning to it here from a slightly different angle: *You must expect that your decisions will give you the results you want. The world gives you what you expect. You're more likely to be right if you expect to be right.*

Each belief causes energy to move in the direction of that belief. Newton's First Law of Motion—an object moving in one direction will continue moving in that direction unless acted on by an external force—applies similarly to the energy generated by thoughts. Thinking you are right is a force that generates momentum. Every outcome is created twice, first in your mind and then in reality. When you expect to be right, you align with the natural energetic forces of life. It requires less energy to confidently believe you are right than to waver between thinking you might be right or wrong.

2. Don't multi-task.

There's no such thing as multitasking. When you think you are multi-tasking, you are giving your attention to a series of tasks, one task at a time, in rapid succession. Therefore, none of the tasks is getting your undivided attention. Stop multitasking.

If you're baking a cake and you take it out of the oven halfway through its cooking time, you'll get a half-baked cake. So, when you're making decisions, and you are partially distracted, you are going to make half-baked decisions. The most common distractions result from phones, computers, tablets, social media, lack of sleep, stress, and poor time management.

Cell phones and other electronic distractions are the most common. Your cell phone is meant to give you access to the world, not for the world to have 24-hour access to you. The following is a four-step strategy to help you break free from internet, phone, and social media addiction:

✓ **Erase the top 3 social media apps that are on your phone for one week.**

Checking your social media regularly is a habit for most. People often check it when they are bored or want to be distracted for a number of several reasons. We must slow the momentum of the habit of checking social media. And you can earn it back.

✓ **Ease Into a Digital Detox**

Begin by gradually reducing your screen time. Start with small, manageable steps, like cutting down screen time by 30 minutes each day and designating two no-tech zones (such as not in the car or during a meeting or class). As you get comfortable, aim for 4–6 hours of daily tech-free time to enjoy a greater sense of freedom and balance.

✓ Set Clear Boundaries

Decide on specific times and spaces where electronics are off-limits, such as no phone use during meals, not using your phone for the first 90 minutes after waking and avoiding it an hour before bed. Setting daily time limits on social media and entertainment apps helps create healthy habits without feeling overwhelmed. During the no-tech periods your phone should either be in a different room or completely turned off. Set to vibrate is not a substitution.

✓ Use Technology to Work for You

Use tech tools to support your goals. Track your screen time, set app usage limits, and enable "Do Not Disturb" during focus periods. Aim to have at least three hours each day without tech interruptions so that your devices serve your priorities rather than distract you.

✓ Earn Your Tech Time

Establish a reward system where phone use is allowed only after productive activities. For example, use your phone only after studying for two hours, completing a work task, or finishing a workout. This approach builds positive habits and reinforces productivity before screen time.

You are the controllable factor; control your electronics habits, and it will be easier for you to train your mind, and you will have greater control of your life.

3 Act on your desired outcome and not on your feelings

Often people spend so much time concerned about how they feel that they don't focus on the outcome itself. There are, of course, settings where feelings are relevant to outcomes, such as healthcare. For instance, in end-of-life care decisions, the outcome of providing the best possible quality of life the feelings and the emotional needs of the patient and family are equally important. However, as it relates to fast decisions most of the time the outcome measure should not be a feeling.

My friend Steve has a 15-year-old son named Jack, who is in 10th grade. Recently, Steve received an e-mail from his son Jack's math teacher stating that Jack had failed the class, and that he had told Jack that the remedy for this failure was that "he needed to work harder and pay more attention."

In Steve's e-mail back to the teacher, he wrote, "If Jack failed the class, you failed him as a teacher. If the measurable outcome of your teaching is how well he did in your class, then you failed. Your solution to Jack failing your class, that he needs to work harder, makes no sense. So please send me a three-step solution for how you and Jack will fix this."

The teacher was offended by the email and decided to involve the principal. The teacher and the principal wanted to speak about the tone and tenor of my friend's e-mail. They wanted to talk about how the email made them feel, but they paid little attention to the measurable outcome. The point of this story is not to be distracted by the way a response made you or someone else feel about the matter but on the outcome needed.

In this example, Steve allowed his email filled with emotions to distract from the desired outcome of a successful outcome for his son. And while the situation worked out in the end it took far longer than needed because of the added distraction.

4 Evaluate your emotions.

Years ago, I worked a shift with a colleague who was clearly in a bad mood, evident by his frown, his tone with staff, and his negative comments to me. During the shift, a family of three who'd been in a car crash arrived. My moody colleague assessed one of them as an urgent care patient, indicating non-life-threatening injuries. The two others he assessed as Alpha traumas. An Alpha trauma activation means that one or more patients are either being transported to the ER or have arrived with life threatening injuries resulting from penetrating or blunt trauma. This triggers the immediate mobilization of a specialized trauma team consisting of a trauma surgeon, emergency medicine physician, trauma nurse, and techs. The goal is to provide immediate coordinated care to maximize the patient's likelihood of surviving.

The moody colleague evaluated this third patient and noticed a "seat belt sign" (indicating potential underlying injuries) during the initial evaluation, took a brief history, and quickly discharged him. The patient later collapsed in the parking lot and was reassessed by another physician, revealing a splenic laceration that required emergency surgery. Afterward, my colleague admitted that his bad mood had adversely affected his judgment.

Afterward, I had a personal, collegial conversation with the treating doctor, and he said, "Being in a cruddy mood did not help matters." Your mood truly matters when you need to make a fast decision. And that is why you need to be able to begin by identifying what you are feeling.

Fast decisions often carry high stakes, and fear is a natural companion in those moments. Yet, it's precisely this fear that underscores the importance of practice—training yourself to act decisively, even in the face of uncertainty. By repeatedly confronting fear, you ensure that when pivotal decisions arise, you meet them head-on, undeterred. As James Neil Hollingworth wisely observed, "Courage is not the absence of fear, but the judgment that something else is more important than fear."

The following are four techniques for identifying major negative emotions and working with them. If you suspect your mood is negative when you need to make a crucial decision, pause and use one of these techniques. To make sure you know how to use them, practice them in low-stakes situations repeatedly so that they'll be available to your muscle memory when the stakes are high.

a) **Quickly Scan your body.** Perform a rapid mental check of your body to identify any areas of tension or discomfort. Pay special attention to common stress points like the neck, shoulders, and jaw. Notice if your hands are sweaty or if your heartbeat is faster than usual.

b) **Label Your Emotion.** Ask yourself, "What am I feeling right now?" The first emotion that comes to mind is your dominant feeling at the moment. For example, it could be anger, sadness, anxiety, or despair. Identifying the emotion is the first step to managing it effectively.

c) **Check Your Thoughts.** Observe your current thoughts. Are they worried, negative, or repetitive? Identifying your thoughts can help you understand the underlying emotions driving them.

d) **Evaluate Behavioral Changes.** Reflect on any recent changes in your behavior. Are you more irritable, withdrawn, or avoiding situations? These behavioral changes can indicate that you are experiencing a dominant negative emotion.

Build your emotional hut before the storm comes. We can be sure that life will cause us to experience negative moods at inopportune times, so we must prepare a few strategies to move ourselves quickly through the negative mood. One such strategy is to create a place in your mind where you can go for solace, comfort, and peace. As John 14:2 says, "My Father's house has many rooms. If it were not so, would I have told you that I am going there to prepare a place for you?" I believe the rooms symbolize places of care and comfort that God always has for you.

Here's how to do it: Imagine your unique heaven on earth, a place of refuge and comfort you can effortlessly access at any moment. It could be a cherished memory, a vivid experience, a happy period of your life, an image, or a beloved person. By anchoring yourself in this heaven on earth, you create an immediate source of solace and happiness that you can draw upon whenever needed.

Those memories of happiness in your life serve as immediate mood changers or mood disruptors that pave the path from a negative mood to a happy mood. Even if the happy feeling is brief, it slows the momentum of the bad mood. So, if you need to make a fast decision, and you've identified that you're in a negative mood, this memory technique will help you clear away the problematic emotions that impede clear decision-making.

Chapter Seven:

Basic Framework for Fast Decisions

"The risk of a wrong decision is preferable to the terror of indecision."

-Maimonides

So far, we've discussed the necessity of making quick decisions under intense conditions and how they shape particular outcomes. Fast decisions are crucial choices made under intense time pressure with significant consequences. Therefore, you must have a clear framework for making these decisions. The framework I have found most reliable is one that I've broken down into a method or formula that is easy to remember: **Time Is Critical—Decide**. The TIC-D method is a structured approach for making fast, effective decisions. Let's break down the process:

1. **Time:**

   ❖ Know how much time you must decide. Time constraints are crucial because they help you focus and prevent overanalyzing or delaying the decision.

❖ Set a clear deadline for when the decision must be made.

2. I = Information:

❖ Within the time you've identified, gather only the essential information. Set a window for gathering this data and stop collecting information once the time limit is up. Too much information can lead to decision paralysis, so prioritize what's relevant to the choice at hand. No matter what, decide based on the information that is available to you.

3. C= Critical Consequences

❖ Assess the potential outcomes of the decision. Weigh these carefully but efficiently, given your time constraints. Is one outcome more important than another? Or is one outcome more catastrophic than another?

4. Decide:

❖ With the time set, information gathered, and consequences considered, it's time to **decide**. Make your decision boldly and act on it. Trust the process you've followed and commit to the execution.

The **TIC-D method** helps streamline decision-making, allowing you to act swiftly and confidently without getting stuck in unnecessary details or second-guessing. This method will require repeated practice, so it will be naturally available to implement when making a fast decision. It is a way of codifying "thin slicing." Thin slicing is a psychological concept popularized by Malcolm Gladwell in his book *Blink: The Power of Thinking Without Thinking*. It is the ability to make quick judgments or inferences about a situation, person, or environment using extremely limited information. TIC-D gives you a set of steps to increase the likelihood that your thin-slicing will be accurate in fast-decision situations.

So, I will share the steps for applying the TIC-D method:

Step 1: Write down the TIC-D 4-step process five times on a piece of paper to commit it to memory.

Step 2: Practice TIC-D in low-consequence situations. For instance, choosing a route to work, buying small household items, making sudden medical decisions, selecting a workout routine, or completing household projects. Start low; expand your reach.

The following is a low-consequence example:

*Scenario:

You've just received an urgent email from your boss while preparing for an important meeting that starts in five minutes. The email asks for immediate feedback on a project that's about to be submitted, and you need to decide how to respond. Your options are:

1. Quickly review the document and provide brief feedback before the meeting.

2. Send a response explaining that you're about to head into a meeting and will provide feedback afterward.

3. Delegate the task to a colleague who is familiar with the project.

You need to make this decision **in less than three minutes** so that you can act accordingly and still be on time for your meeting.

Steps for the Practice Session:

1. **Time (30 seconds)**

   ❖ **Set a time limit**: You only have five minutes, so it's essential to determine how much time to spend on each step quickly.

   ❖ **Action**: Acknowledge that you must decide within the next **two-and-a-half minutes**. This creates urgency and helps you stay focused on finding a quick solution.

2. **Information (1 minute)**

   ❖ **Gather essential information**: Quickly review the email and the attached document (if any) to understand what your boss is asking for and assess whether you have enough time to provide meaningful feedback.

   ❖ **Action**: Spend **one minute** reviewing the following:

      ▪ The **urgency** of the feedback (is it a final review or just a quick glance?).

      ▪ The **length and complexity** of the document (can you skim it, or does it require deep analysis?).

- **Your current schedule** (how much time is left before your meeting?).

This short window allows you to quickly assess what's being asked and whether you can handle it in the time that is available.

3. **Consequences (1 minute)**

   - ❖ **Assess the consequences**: Think about the outcomes of each option. Consider the importance of the project, your relationship with your boss, and the impact of delaying or delegating the task.

   - ❖ **Action**: Spend **one minute** weighing the consequences of each option:

     - **Option 1** (Quick feedback): You'll provide some input, but it might be rushed and less thorough.

     - **Option 2** (Delay feedback): You'll be honest about your time constraints, which might delay the project submission.

     - **Option 3** (Delegate): A colleague can handle it, but you must trust their judgment and clearly communicate the request.

4. **Decide (30 seconds)**

   - ❖ **Make your decision**: With the information and consequences in mind, decide which course of action is best and act immediately.

   - ❖ **Action**: Spend the remaining **30 seconds** making the decision and executing it. Act decisively, whether it's reviewing the document quickly, replying to your boss with an explanation, or delegating to a colleague. If you choose to delegate, communicate the task and its urgency.

Debrief:

Reflect on the process:

❖ How did setting a strict time limit affect your decision-making process?

❖ Did the quick information-gathering give you enough clarity to make a confident decision?

❖ How did considering the consequences help you feel more assured in your choice?

❖ How did you feel after making the final decision and taking action within three minutes?

This short reflection helps you evaluate how effectively you applied the TIC-D method under tight time constraints.

This practice session simulates a situation many professionals face—deciding how to respond to an urgent work request under time pressure. Practicing the **TIC-D method** in a three-to-five-minute scenario can improve your ability to make quick, well-informed decisions without overthinking or hesitation.

Training in these fast-paced situations will enhance your confidence and efficiency in handling high-pressure decisions in the workplace and other areas of life. The goal is to get used to deploying the TIC-D technique. Use it three times per week so that it becomes automatic. And learn what adjustments you need to make when there are no significant consequences.

First Decision, Best Decision

When in doubt, know that your first decision will usually be your best—unless significant new information becomes known after you've made that first choice. Why? Because your subconscious is always working and stores every experience you've had. It has access to information you have consciously forgotten, and that subconscious information will inform your first decision, even though you don't know it.

In 1994, Researchers Antoine Bechara, Antonio Damasio, Hanna Damasio, and Steven Anderson developed the **Iowa Gambling Task** assessment tool at the University of Iowa. This psychological assessment evaluates decision-making abilities by simulating real-life risk and reward scenarios. The researchers demonstrated the validity of trusting one's first decision.

In the Iowa Gambling Task, each participant is presented with four decks of virtual cards on a computer screen. Each card in each deck will cause you to either win a certain amount of money or lose a certain amount. The participants are told that the goal is to win as much money as possible. They do not know that two decks will produce winning results while the other two will produce losing results.

Participants must choose one card at a time from any of the four decks. Each time they choose a card, they know immediately whether it is a winning or losing card. Decks A and B have $100 worth of winning cards and $300 worth of losing cards. Decks C and have $50 worth of winning and $100 worth of losing cards. In short, decks C and D are more advantageous and will result in the largest gains throughout the experiment. Each participant is also connected to a monitor that measures sweat production, which will increase in response to stress.

It took healthy participants between 40 and 50 card selections on average before determining which decks were favorable. All participants were definitive about which decks were more favorable by card number 80.

However, the researchers noticed something interesting. When the participants got to the tenth card in one of the unfavorable decks, their skin electrodes showed increased sweat production. An entire 70 cards earlier than when all of them consciously knew it was an unfavorable deck. This means the participants subconsciously figured out the pattern long before their conscious minds got it.

In short, our subconscious minds tend to synthesize more information and know its impact sooner than our conscious minds. Thus, in a situation where you are unsure how to decide, trust that your subconscious is already at work and go with your first decision, which is likely to be the optimal one.

Chapter Eight:

———≋———

Decisions Are Emotional

"Nothing is wrong at this moment, even if it feels like everything's falling apart. If you sense your life's a mess right now, this is simply because your fears are just a little stronger than your faith."
—*Robin Sharma, The 5 AM Club*

In chapter five, we discussed the value of recognizing and working with negative emotions as you prepare to make fast decisions and while making them. This chapter will analyze the emotional component of making fast decisions.

Decisions are driven by emotions. Many studies have shown that emotions influence how we make decisions. It's hard to pinpoint an exact percentage because our minds are complex, and everyone is different. However, research in various fields, including neuroscience, economics, business, medicine, and psychology, suggests that about 95% of our decisions are emotional.

Neuroscientists, for example, have studied how emotions shape our preferences, guide risk assessment, and influence judgments about rewards and consequences. For example,

Antonio Damasio's research revealed that patients with brain lesions affecting emotional processing had difficulty making decisions, even though their cognitive abilities were intact.

Daniel Kahneman and Amos Tversky's research demonstrated that cognitive biases and heuristics, influenced by emotions, often cause people to make irrational decisions. Their work highlights how mental shortcuts, like availability or anchoring heuristics, can lead to systematic judgment errors, especially under uncertainty or risk.

Risk Tolerance and Risk Aversion

Let's start with two broad categories of uncertainty that arise in decision-making: **aversion and tolerance**. In any decision, you are likely to be driven more by either aversion to a negative outcome or attraction to a positive outcome. In decision-making, these two distinct mindset types are risk aversion and risk tolerance. Understanding which of these two mindsets drives you is key to understanding how to use your emotions best to arrive at the optimal choice.

People with a risk-averse mindset are more concerned with avoiding potential losses; they tend to favor the security of smaller, guaranteed benefits over bigger but less certain gains. They are more driven by the fear of losing something than by the possible joy of gaining something. Consequently, those who tend to be risk-averse are more likely to accept lower returns if they are guaranteed rather than gambling on higher rewards that are uncertain. This cautious approach pervades all areas of the life of risk-averse, from how they manage their finances and make career moves to everyday personal choices such as staying at the same stable job over a high-paying but uncertain opportunity. Or, while at a restaurant, choose the dish they had before instead of trying a new exotic option on the menu that might be more adventurous but could also be something they don't enjoy.

People with a more risk-tolerant mindset accept uncertainty and the potential for loss as part of the journey towards achieving bigger rewards. These individuals are comfortable facing challenges and see risks as required elements for valuable opportunities. Their decision-making process leans towards options that might carry a higher level of unpredictability, motivated by the expectation of substantial gains. This mindset, too, influences various life decisions, from financial investments to career paths and personal development, leading the risk-tolerant to choose more aggressive strategies.

While some of us tend to be more risk-averse and others more risk-tolerant, we can be one or the other, depending on the situation. Our brains have distinct neuropathways for processing risk-averse and risk-tolerant behaviors. Recognizing which mode you are in can significantly enhance your decision-making effectiveness.

Signs of Risk-Avoidant Behavior:

1. **Preferring Safety:** You often opt for familiar situations to minimize potential harm or loss.

2. **Fear of Failure:** You shy away from challenges or opportunities that involve uncertainty and potential setbacks.

3. **Indecisiveness:** You experience hesitation and reluctance when faced with choices that carry even a moderate level of risk.

4. **Resistance to Change:** You feel uncomfortable with unfamiliar or unpredictable situations that deviate from your established routines.

5. **Overestimation of Risks:** You tend to focus on the likelihood and consequences of negative outcomes; this leads to a tendency to avoid opportunities with perceived risks.

6. **Seeking Reassurance:** You crave validation from others before making decisions, needing confirmation to alleviate your anxieties about potential risks.

7. **Conservative Approach:** You prefer caution and incremental progress, overtaking bold or innovative actions that may involve greater uncertainty.

Recognize when you're avoiding risks and decide if it truly benefits you or if you need to change your mindset.

Signs of Risk-Tolerant Behavior

1. **Embracing Challenges:** You tend to view difficulties as opportunities for growth and innovation rather than sources of fear or uncertainty.

2. **Adventurous Spirit:** You often seek out new experiences and ventures, even if they entail a degree of uncertainty or potential risk.

3. **Confidence in Decision-Making:** You trust your judgment and intuition to manage uncertain situations and make bold choices.

4. **Openness to Change:** You see novelty as an opportunity for learning and advancement rather than a threat to stability or security.

5. **Optimistic Outlook:** You focus on the potential rewards and opportunities associated with taking calculated risks rather than dwelling on potential setbacks or failures.

6. **Toughness in the Face of Failure:** You view setbacks as valuable learning experiences and opportunities for growth rather than insurmountable obstacles.

7. **Comfort with Uncertainty:** You are comfortable venturing into the unknown and adapting to changing circumstances with agility and confidence.

Recognizing these signs can help you use your risk tolerance to pursue opportunities, overcome challenges, and confidently achieve your goals.

In short, recognizing whether you're in a **risk-avoidant** or **risk-tolerant** mindset empowers you to make intentional internal adjustments. By identifying which approach best aligns with your goals for a specific decision, you take a major leap forward in improving your decision-making process. Understanding and adapting to the mindset that serves you best is a meaningful change, setting you up for success with every choice you face!

Context matters. The time of day, for example, plays a significant role in risk tolerance. Your levels of serotonin—a chemical neurotransmitter that helps regulate your mood and cognitive functioning, also known as "the feel-good transmitter"—are at their peak in the morning and can make you more receptive to new ideas. So, you're likely to be more risk-tolerant in the morning. Later in the day, as serotonin levels drop, a shift towards a risk-averse mindset may occur, necessitating a decision-making strategy that emphasizes comfort and familiarity.

The Twenty-Seven Emotions That Can Affect Your Decisions

The key to making fast decisions is not overloading the rational mind with data but tapping into the emotions that guide your choices. By tuning into these emotional undercurrents and adjusting your approach accordingly, you can significantly enhance your ability to decide efficiently and effectively.

A study led by psychologist Dacher Keltner at the University of California, Berkeley, and published in 2017 expanded the traditional understanding of human emotions beyond the basic ones—happiness, sadness, anger, surprise, fear, and disgust—and identified a list of 27 distinct emotions: admiration, adoration, aesthetic appreciation, amusement, anger, anxiety, awe, awkwardness, boredom, calmness, confusion, craving, disgust, empathic pain, entrancement, envy, excitement, fear, horror, interest, joy, nostalgia, relief, romance, sadness, satisfaction, and surprise.

These 27 can be grouped into positive and negative emotions. Positive emotion is a feel-good sensation that lifts our spirits, boosts our happiness, and contributes to our overall sense of fulfillment. They often emerge from rewarding experiences or from looking forward to good things happening. These emotions encourage you to chase your dreams, deepen your connections with others, and build your capacity to cope with stress. The positive emotions from Keltner's list include admiration, adoration, aesthetic appreciation, amusement, awe, calmness, excitement, joy, romance, and surprise.

Negative emotions can lower your spirits and undermine your well-being. They usually come about when we have faced, are facing, or anticipate challenges, threats, or setbacks. Despite being unpleasant, negative emotions play a critical role in your survival by urging you to tackle problems, safeguard yourself from harm, and adapt your behavior to avoid similar issues in the future. Learning to navigate and understand these emotions requires personal development and emotional awareness. Negative emotions from Keltner's list include anxiety, anger, awkwardness, boredom, confusion, craving, envy, fear, horror, and sadness.

Esther and Jerry Hicks, authors of the book, *Ask and It Is Given,* propose a unique way to frame the emotions that is complementary to Keltner's in their book. They ranked the emotions from the highest or most positive vibration to the lowest or most negative and created 22 positive and negative emotions that affect our decision-making:

1. Joy, Love, Appreciation, Freedom, Empowerment,

2. Passion

3. Enthusiasm/Eagerness/Happiness

4. Positive Expectations/Belief

5. Optimism

6. Hopefulness

7. Contentment

8. Boredom

9. Pessimism

10. Frustration/Irritation/Impatience

11. Overwhelmed

12. Disappointment

13. Doubt

14. Worry

15. Blame

16. Discouragement

17. Anger

18. Revenge

19. Hatred/Rage

20. Jealousy

21. Insecurity/Guilt/Unworthiness

22. Fear/Grief/Depression/Despair/Powerlessness

Twenty-seven Emotions, or Only Two?

Instead of 27 or 22 human emotions, they can all be consolidated into two: love and fear. As shown in Psalm 136:5-9, love is a part of natural creation: "Who by his understanding made the heavens, His love endures forever. Who spread out the earth upon the waters, His love endures forever. Who made the great lights—His love endures forever. The sun governs the day, and His love endures forever. The moon and stars govern the night; His love endures forever."

And since love was woven into the fabric of creation, it has always been present. Hence, fear was created so that we could experience love. If you only know love and have nothing else to compare it to, do you really know what love is? Is there a genuine recognition of love's depth? However, if you have something to contrast love to, like fear, you can fully appreciate the embodiment of what love is.

Emotions like happiness and joy are vibrant expressions of love, radiating its pure essence. In contrast, emotions like sadness and anger are echoes of fear, shadows that trace back to their looming presence.

From a spiritual perspective, the coexistence of love and fear can be viewed as a fundamental aspect of the human experience, designed to foster growth, learning, and evolution at a spiritual level. In many cultures, love is considered the highest vibration, energy, ultimate truth, and the essence of the divine or the universe itself. It represents unity, connection, and the inherent oneness of all beings. Love is seen as the soul's natural state, an eternal force that binds the fabric of the universe together.

Fear, in contrast, is a lower vibration, a product of the ego or the illusion of being separate from others or a higher reality. It arises from the perceived disconnection from the divine, others, and even our true selves. Fear emerges when we forget our true nature, which is love. One way of thinking about it is that love is light or the sun. It is natural and always present. Fear, then, would represent a lack of light. When we are afraid, we need to let in light.

Humans are hard-wired to understand our experiences through comparisons. If you only know love and have nothing to contrast it with, do you know what love is? Is there genuine appreciation? I suggest that fear be created to experience love.

I experienced this vividly one scorching summer day while working in a rural ER in Maryland. I remember being in a happy mood. And then we got a call on the EMS emergency radio. The paramedic said in a panicked voice, "We have a nine-year-old girl who was found at the bottom of the pool. She is unconscious. We are unable to intubate the patient because of too much fluid. We are three to five minutes away." I responded, "Put her on 100% oxygen; see you when you get here."

I went to the other end of the ER to let the charge nurse, Leah, know what was coming in. Leah was a 60-year-old, hard-nosed, excellent nurse who had been working in ERs for 40 years. By the time I got back, the crew was already in the trauma bay, transferring the nine-year-old patient—I'll call her Hannah—to our hospital stretcher.

Her skin had a greyish hue. She lay there listlessly, pigtails and all. Fluid was coming out of all orifices. This was when I needed to snap into action. But fear welled up in me, and I froze. I had been an emergency medicine doctor for 10 years and had never frozen before that moment. The difference was that Hannah was the first trauma pediatric patient I'd encountered since the birth of my daughter 11 months earlier.

Leah, the hard-nosed nurse, understood instantly what was happening. She nudged me and said, "You can think about your daughter later. Get going." I snapped out of it enough to order an intubation set-up, which included all the equipment needed for endotracheal intubation. This would open the airway, allowing us to help Hannah breathe and give medications or suction material from the lungs. One tech started an IV on the left arm, while a second tech started an IV on the right arm.

I asked the clerk to get someone from the Children's Trauma Center on the line and transfer the call to the trauma bay. Experts in pediatric trauma medicine staffed this hospital, which is 35 miles away. She had already called and told me she was on hold,

I attempted to intubate, but because of all the fluid Hannah had aspirated in the pool, I couldn't see her windpipe, also known as the trachea. The respiratory therapist turned the suction up to clear the fluid. I still couldn't see her cords, which would help guide the tube into her trachea. Her oxygen saturation fell from the 80s to the 70s (98 to 100 is normal). We tried more suction, and then we tried positive pressure ventilation to push air into her lungs. Another trauma team member got another suction catheter. Now, two team members were each holding a suction catheter down her throat. I said, "Ready? Go." We could suction a lot of fluid fast so that I could see the cords. Bam! I placed the tube.

The oxygen saturation only reached the low 80s, causing me to be on high alert. And there was fluid coming out of the tube. One of the respiratory therapists said that he had just read a medical journal article about "placing drowning patients on their stomachs when trying to ventilate..." I had never heard of such a thing. I thought, "How would it look if I did this new maneuver that is not the gold standard of care, and the patient died?"—a very risk-averse thought. Yet, here was Hannah in front of me, slowly dying.

At that moment, the clerk yelled, "The Children's Center trauma doctor is on the phone." Before I took the call, I agreed with the respiratory therapist and directed the team to turn the patient onto her stomach.

I went to the phone about five feet from where Hannah was on the gurney and told the Children's trauma doctor the situation. He was a slow-talking, calm, older physician. He began to offer recommendations. The first was to change the settings on the ventilator. No change. Increase the oxygen. Still no change. Turn the patient on her stomach for better oxygenation of her lungs. Already did it. My back-and-forth went on for ten minutes with the team trying everything, with no substantive improvements.

The Children's doctor asked if I could transfer the patient to the Children's Trauma Center. Hannah's breathing and vital signs were so unstable that I did not think she would make it, but I said yes. While we talked, he had already dispatched the helicopter and told me it would be there in two minutes.

When I re-evaluated Hannah, her blood pressure was lower, and her saturations were 79 – 80%. She was getting worse. So, I changed my mind about transferring Hannah and asked the clerk to get the trauma doctor back on the phone. But then I heard the helicopter landing and something inside me said to transfer this patient. I knew that I had maximized my medical knowledge as it related to her care.

The helicopter paramedics flew the nine-year-old to the pediatric trauma medical center, and the ER team received word that she was in critical condition but improving. One of the doctors reminded me that drownings with unknown submersion, or downtime, where the patient is found unconscious, have a 90% one-year mortality.

On follow-up, Hannah was discharged from the hospital a month later, fully neurologically intact, and was expected to live a normal life. That morning, after we transferred Hannah, I talked with her mother. She cried in my arms and said, "I had just fussed at her this morning and told her that she may have to go live with her father because her mouth was getting too smart."

Did she go on to have a more profound appreciation of her child and greater patience for the ebbs and flows of raising an adolescent? I would like to believe she did.

Hannah's mother's response that morning highlights how fear can make us recognize and feel our love more sharply.

Managing Fear

But fear can also negatively impact any area of your life if you allow it to. It happened to me for a moment Hannah arrived in the ER, and I'm forever grateful to Leah for instantaneously diagnosing my problem and snapping me out of it.

Fear is by far the biggest culprit when it comes to interfering with or disrupting decision making. It can paralyze your judgment and hold you back from action. It is especially insidious when you need to make fast decisions. It can cloud your judgment, leading you down paths of uncertainty. Simply recognizing fear's immense impact gives you great power. Being able to call it what it is pulls it out of the shadows and allows you to face it head-on.

Acknowledge fear, but move past it. Don't be overwhelmed by it. God did not give you the spirit of fear. Fear only exists in your mind because you allow it to. Often, what is feared is greater in your mind than in reality. The truth is every single person— big, small, strong, weak, old, young, rich, or poor, brave, scared, powerful, educated, less educated, healthy, sick, wise, confident, ordinary, privileged, tough, quiet, hardworking, outspoken — experiences various degrees of fear at times.

However, babies experience the least fear. Why? As previously stated, fear is a learned behavior. You were born with only two natural fears: the fear of loud noises and the fear of falling. All other fears are learned, which means they can be unlearned.

Fear may feel justified in certain situations—like the fear I felt transferring Hanah, knowing she could have died en route. This may be thought of as a healthy fear. But even when fear seems rational or shared by others, it does not excuse inaction. You must act decisively, make critical decisions, and move forward, no matter how heavy fear feels. Push through it. Most fears you face today are within your power to conquer, and you are responsible for overcoming them. Fear cannot and will not dictate your actions.

Conversely, sometimes, feared outcomes become a reality. A career setback, loss of a loved one, financial crisis, wayward child, a breakup, or public failure—these moments can be gut-wrenching, overwhelming, and painful. But here's the truth: enduring hardship is part of life, and you can handle it. The most important question isn't, "Why me?" but "What will I do next?"

You get back up. You learn the lessons life is teaching you, even through the pain. Yes, you might need a moment to pause and "lick your wounds," to grieve, or to heal—that's fine; you are human. But never stop moving forward. Pain isn't a punishment; it is an experience that gives you an opportunity to grow. It's part of the price of living a meaningful life.

Unlearning fears

1. Acknowledge and identify your fear: Recognizing what you are afraid of is the first step.

2. Educate and self-assess: Is this a fear of an outcome that can really happen? Is it based on a genuine experience?

Is it an irrational belief? For instance, are clowns real? Does the boogeyman really exist?

Understanding its origin helps you separate it from your present reality. Learning more about the feared object or situation will help dispel myths and reduce irrational fears.

3. Challenge the Fear

 ❖ Question the rationality of fear. Ask:

   ▪ Is this fear realistic or exaggerated?

   ▪ What evidence supports or contradicts it?

   ▪ What is the worst that could happen, and how likely is that outcome?

4. Face your fear in controlled, manageable steps. Gradual exposure reduces its power over time. Start small, begin with less intimidating exposures and gradually increase the level of exposure as you become more comfortable. For example, if you are afraid of clowns, start by looking at pictures, then viewing clowns on videos and finally going to go visit a clown.

5. Replace Fearful Thoughts

 ❖ Practice positive self-talk and affirmations to counteract fear-driven narratives. Replace "This is too hard" with "No one better than me."

 ❖ Visualization: See yourself conquering the very situations that once triggered fear. Picture every detail of your triumph. Positive mental imagery isn't just a tool—it's your blueprint for rewiring your brain and building unshakable confidence.

6. Build Coping Mechanisms

Develop techniques to manage fear's physical and emotional symptoms:

1. **Breathing Exercises:** Deep, controlled breaths calm your nervous system.

2. **Mindfulness or Meditation:** These practices help you stay grounded in the present moment.

3. **Physical Activity:** Exercise can reduce anxiety and build resilience.

7. Develop Coping Mechanisms

❖ **Control Your Breath:** Use deep, steady breathing to calm your nervous system instantly.

❖ **Ground Your Mind:** Practice mindfulness or meditation to stay present and focused.

❖ **Strengthen Your Body:** Use the power of physical activity to reduce anxiety and build resilience.

What I feared didn't break me—it built me. It pushed me forward. It made me sharp. Growing up with a stutter wasn't just a challenge—it became my training ground. Every word came with the potential to stutter. And thus create a battlefield for me. If I slipped, the bullies would pounce. I learned to speak in succinct, deliberate sentences. This sharpened my quick-thinking skills.

So, I adapted. I learned to speak with power—succinct, deliberate, unstoppable.

The struggle became my edge. It forged my critical thinking and decision-making under pressure. That edge led me to major in mathematics, master problem-solving, and ultimately walk into the high-stakes world of emergency medicine—where every second counts and every word can save a life. Fear didn't hold me back. It made me fearless.

Be patient and persistent. Overcoming fear takes time and effort, so stay committed and don't get discouraged. Fear, when faced and reframed, can become the foundation of your greatest strength.

Chapter Nine:

Growing In The Grey Area

"The quality of your life is in direct proportion to the amount of uncertainty you can comfortably deal with."

-Tony Robbins

Not all decisions are created equal. They're not all cut and dried. Many of the most important decisions lie in the grey area—where things are ambiguous, uncertain, complex, and even scary. It's where you're just not sure, where there's no clear right or wrong answer, and the best course of action is not obvious. There are numerous factors to consider—potential risks and multiple outcomes. This is where you need to become comfortable and skilled. The grey area is where you win and where you move toward greatness.

In the grey area of decision-making, you may encounter:

- ❖ Uncertain consequences of your choices
- ❖ Complex or ambiguous circumstances or austere environments
- ❖ Divergent opinions and facts that do not align.

❖ Moral or ethical questions that aren't clear-cut.

❖ Lack of adequate information or data

In business and life, there are grey-area decisions. There are certainly grey-area moments in the ER. There was one such moment in an ER in the Midwest. Here's Bill's story:

Bill's patient chart immediately caught my attention when I read the phrase "penile ring." Hmm, what did that mean? Bill was a healthy-appearing 25-year-old with multiple tattoos and a few nose rings and earrings. Upon examination, Bill appeared anxious, so I asked him how I could help.

He said, "Doc, I am okay. My blood pressure is a little high. If you give me something for it, I can leave." I looked at the chart and saw "penile ring" again. I informed Bill that I could fix his blood pressure, and I asked if he would like me to look at the ring. Often patients appreciate you taking the onus off them. He was relieved that I had cut to the chase.

Bill lifted his gown, and there was a one-inch-thick steel ring at the base of his penis. He had somehow lowered the ring down over the tip of his penis and wedged it behind his testicles. He could not get it off. Clinically, I assessed both the penis and testicles, and both had appropriate color, warmth, sensation, and appeared normal. Bill was still quite anxious. While assessing his testicles, the nurse and I attempted to slip the ring off. No luck. I must add that it is common for patients to come to the ER with all types of objects, instruments, and tools stuck in, on, or through various body parts. This was one that I had not seen before.

The nurse and I obtained lubricant and soap and attempted to remove the ring. Again, no luck. Bill said that he could do it himself now that we had lubricated the area. He was not successful. I called the hospital engineering department to see if we could obtain bolt cutters or any instrument that could be of assistance. Someone from engineering came to the ER with a few gadgets, but again, no luck. The ring was one-inch-thick steel. Bill's anxiety increased.

By now, the charge nurse, the nurse, the float nurse, and the tech assigned to the patient were all involved in the patient's care. Other staff had also started coming into the room under the guise of needing something from that room, but many were just gawking. At one point, I insisted that any personnel not involved in the patient's care not enter the treatment room.

Early in the process, I contacted the urology service in case we needed their expertise on the male reproductive system. They arrived just as the engineers were considering which tools to use. The urology attending tried more lubricant and aggressive attempts to remove the ring. The manipulation became too painful for Bill. We tried giving him pain medicine, and still, the manipulation was too painful. Bill's genital area had become swollen and had turned dark red. Urology suggested that they may need to take Bill to the operating room to remove the penile ring under general anesthesia. However, the urology doctor said, "I do not think that we have any instruments that are strong enough to cut the ring."

To my surprise, Bill announced, "I am going home with the ring on." I tried for fifteen minutes to talk him into not leaving.

By the time we finished talking, his testicles and penis were starting to turn blue, a sign of a lack of blood flow and a true medical emergency. Bill began to remove the monitoring devices hooked up to his chest. He got up and started looking for his clothes. To my professional and personal amazement, he was seriously going home.

I had an anxious 25-year-old healthy male with blue testicles and a blue penis who now wants to leave. I explained to Bill that the prolonged lack of blood supply to his testicles would cause them to become permanently damaged and that we needed to fix this now. I paged for a psychiatric consultant to assess Bill's competence to make his own decisions, but that consult took a long time to come to the room and evaluate him. I am sure many would suggest he had the right to go home on some modern-day ethical spectrum, and I couldn't stop him. Yet, going through my mind was that if I let Bill leave, his penis and testicles were going to become ischemic and cause severe tissue damage. The damage could cause an infection that would travel into his bloodstream, also known as sepsis. This could kill him, or the tissue damage alone could lead to the need to amputate his penis, which would change his life forever.

I was 100 percent certain that Bill would choose not to leave if the current circumstances did not stress him. This was truly a grey area. Based on existing policy and protocols, I would not have been wrong to allow Bill to leave. However, if Bill were my son, I would not let him go, and I would not want any other treatment provider to let him leave.

Acting in the best interest of the patient. I assessed clinically that he was a threat to himself and should not leave. So, I injected him with medicine that made him go to sleep. When he was asleep, we once more attempted to remove the ring. By now, his penis and testicles were very swollen, and even with moderate sedation, our attempts were causing the patient a great deal of pain. At one point, the urologist proposed trying to saw off the ring with a hack saw. The problem was that with one wrong movement, the saw could lacerate or cut off part of his genital area. I could not allow such a risk.

Meanwhile, the penis and testicles were turning increasingly blue, indicating further decreasing blood circulation to his genital area. We decided that we would deeply sedate Bill so that he would not feel any pain when we manipulated his testicles. And this would require me to intubate him.

The Stakes Are Too High

I set up for intubation. We used our standard protocols for Rapid Sequence Intubation (RSI). When using RSI, a clinician typically gives medicines that are an anesthetic, a sedative, and a muscular paralytic. The paralytic does exactly what it says: it paralyzes the patient's muscles so that he or she can't move, including not being able to use his or her respiratory muscles to breathe. This is done so that the clinician can put the endotracheal tube into the patient's trachea to breathe for the patient if the patient can no longer breathe on their own once the RSI medications are given, the tube should be in place in less than thirty seconds after the medications or the patient will suffocate.

Some patients have what we call a difficult airway, and the clinician may not realize it until after the RSI medicines have been given. Bill had a difficult airway, and I was having difficulty placing the endotracheal tube. Rarely do I have difficulty. As I had done when I'd encountered other difficult airways, I started to pray as I was working.

"Lord, this man was healthy when he came in here. 'It is not my will but thy will.' But Lord, please help me maneuver this tube in his airway. Keep me calm and faithful, most Holy One; please continue to bless me, most Holy One. I do not know anything about this man, but I imagine that he has a family who loves him, who wants to see him home tonight. Most Mighty Father, please forgive me for being so selfish, but this man trusted me. I know that whatever happens here is your will, but please, don't let this man die today. Please help me get this tube in his trachea. You are the most powerful. I know you bless who you want to bless. You do what you want to do and when you want to do it. If I could just call on you and humbly ask you to show me your favor once again. I submit to you, Lord, that you are the most powerful. I am nothing. I am just an innocent morsel who is trying to be your servant. I beg you, Lord, to please take time, and grant me my selfish request. You always take care of me, most Heavenly Father. I ask this from you in the Lord's name. Amen."

Apart from the sweat on my forehead, the nurses and tech involved could not tell how scared I was. Later, they commented that I appeared calm and relaxed. I had practiced keeping my voice even toned and my movements slow and deliberate during stressful cases. I think this is called equanimity under pressure. The truth is, these kinds of cases make you grow hair on your chest. Just as I finished the prayer, I was able to put the tube in Bill's trachea. Bill's pulse oxygen never dropped below 94 percent. Placing the trach tube took about 40 seconds.

Now that we had Bill heavily sedated, we again attempted to manipulate the penile ring out from behind his testicles and penis. No luck. I decided to call the local fire department and ask if they could come and help. I knew the hospital was going to frown on the fact that I called, but I was out of options for help from inside our walls. We could hear the sirens and trucks from blocks away. They arrived about six minutes later. I did not expect two fire trucks and a supervisor's truck. The commander and a few firefighters came in, and from his perspective, it looked as if we were going to try to use the big bolt cutters to get the ring off. The commander said, "Stop, don't do anything else; we can fix this. We had a similar case at another hospital last week."

They returned from their truck with a small electric hand saw and a curved piece of metal about one inch wide and three inches long, attached to a long metal rod. At this point, everybody working in the ER was trying to figure out a way to come in and see what was happening. While I was managing the situation, the nursing supervisor for the entire hospital came and told me that I was "not supposed to call the firefighters, and I should have called the environmental services supervisor." I told her "Thank you for the advice and please step out of the code resuscitation room." She continued to want to discuss the patient I was treating, but there was no time for distractions. I turned my back and went back to taking care of Bill. She was in administrator mode; I was in saving a patient's life mode. The truth is I was the accountable doctor for Bill and would have called anyone who I thought could help.

One of the firefighters applied a special type of lubrication and slid the curved metal contraption between the ring and Bill's testicles. He then used the modified hand saw to begin to cut the ring. It had a special guard on it to keep the blade from suddenly pressing down. The curved contraption served as the guard to protect the genital area. The firefighter turned on the saw and began cutting.

The next thing I heard was "damn" from the firefighter who had been cutting the ring. He said, "The ring is thick, I broke the blade … I have to get a new blade." He went to his truck, returned, and started to cut once again. After a few minutes, he stopped—the second blade had broken. He went back to his truck and, this time, came back with a different, modified handheld device. He began to cut again, and after a few more minutes, he could cut all the way through the ring. He was then able to manipulate a device to help pry the ring open, and it was off.

Bill's genitals started to show signs of positive blood flow. The urologist assessed him again. We stopped the sedation and removed the endotracheal tube. Bill woke up. Due in part to the sedation, he was calmer. He thanked us profusely. We observed him for three more hours, and then I discharged him. I knew there would be gawkers, and he did not need to feel their eyes judging him as he left, so I let him leave through the exit that usually only ambulance crew members use instead of walking through the main clinical area past everyone.

Grey Areas

There were many grey areas in my treatment of Bill, decisions that did not have clear outcomes and that had an enormous impact on Bill's life.

Here are all the grey-area decisions I made:

1. Using lubricants further irritated the area after I had already attempted this.

2. Calling engineering for bolt cutters.

3. Calling urology versus calling plastics or trauma surgery.

4. Allowing the urology doctor to attempt to manipulate the testicles again.

5. Paging the psychiatric service.

6. Preventing him from leaving—even when he wanted to leave—by giving him a light sleeping medicine.

7. Intubating him

8. Using a paralytic to intubate Bill.

9. Attempting to manipulate his genitals again after he was sedated.

10. Calling the fire department and allowing firefighters to work on the patient.

11. Discharging Bill after he'd been sedated.

12. Letting Bill go out of the ambulance exit.

How should you make decisions where there is a lot of grey area? You can follow your gut, also known as your instinct, also known as your subconscious intuition—which, as we discussed above, will likely supply you with knowledge you are not consciously aware of. You can follow existing procedures and protocols. You can decide based on the path of least resistance. But often, the path of least resistance is not the right; it's just the one that requires the least effort or thought on your part. Often, it is as simple as exercising good judgment. How will you decide on grey areas? The following is a template for operating in the grey area, using my ER story to illustrate.

Five questions to ask when you are deciding in the grey area:

1. Who are my decisions expected to serve? Me? Someone else? Or both?"

2. Who will benefit or be harmed by my decision? How much and for how long?

   ❖ In my case, it was the patient.

3. Given the reality of the situation, what are my options?

   ❖ Often, you inadvertently try to make decisions based on ideal conditions rather than the actual realities. It's crucial to tailor and adjust your decisions and actions according to the current context, constraints, and probabilities of the situation at hand. With Bill's surgery, I couldn't just check the correct box; I had to think outside it.

4. What decisions am I willing to accept and stand by?

❖ To answer this question, you need to do a pre-mortem. Imagine explaining your decision to a loved one or a mentor whose opinion you deeply value. Reflect on what they might think about your choice. While what other people think about you is none of your business because you can't control their thoughts, the reality is that everyone has a few people whose opinions they care about.

5. How do my core values influence this decision? And should my beliefs impact this decision?

❖ What do you stand for?

▪ I am a doctor and have taken a vow to do no harm. I also believe I should do my part to change the world for the better. I changed the world of this patient by aligning my decision with my core belief that his life mattered just as much as my own.

Two challenging elements of making high-stakes grey area choices is that what you believe to be the right decision may not be viewed that way by others, and not every one of the decisions will give you the results you expected. Even then—especially then—you must continue to practice making grey area decisions, learning as well as you can from your mistakes.

Chapter Ten:

—⁓—

Blind Spots and Psychological Traps

*"The first principle is that you must not fool yourself—
and you are the easiest person to fool."*
-Richard P. Feynman

Often, our minds dwell on specific decisions and their outcomes, especially when they do not yield the expected or desired results. This leads us to scrutinize the information we rely on and sometimes question the intentions of those involved. However, we often overlook the importance of introspection. Self-reflection after a decision is crucial—not to assign blame, but to help us view our actions through a lens of learning and self-improvement. Here are three questions to ask after you decide:

1. How did my past experiences shape this decision?

2. Did external factors influence me more than they should have been allowed to?

3. Did the desire to conform and the fear of being different sway my judgment?

Asking these questions regularly after you make decisions will reveal that past decisions often create mental shortcuts for similar future decisions. These shortcuts, known as heuristics, should be evaluated to help us understand their origins and assess their effectiveness in our decision-making process.

Be mindful of potential biases embedded in your heuristics. When a decision leads to the desired outcome, you might assume your decision-making method or your heuristic were effective. However, considering all contributing factors, not just the decision and the result, is essential.

Let's say you saw several plane crashes on the news in the months leading up to your family's trip to Disney World and chose to cancel the trip because "there have been so many plane crashes lately." This decision is less than optimal because one plane crash does not increase the probability of another.

The way to enable heuristics to work in your favor is to understand and avoid psychological decision traps. A psychological decision trap is a rule of thumb we use to streamline our decision-making efforts, but which contains biases.

Being aware of the most common psychological traps, even just a little, can significantly reduce their impact on your decisions. By recognizing your biases, you can make more informed and balanced decisions. The following are the seven biases that are most likely to affect your decision-making.

1. Anchoring

Anchoring is a cognitive bias where the first piece of information we receive heavily influences our subsequent decisions, often subconsciously or unknowingly. This initial information serves as a reference point, or anchor, against which we compare and assess all later information.

For example, suppose you're trying to decide how much to pay for a new car. And the salesperson starts by suggesting a much higher than market price, say $30,000. Even if it's negotiable, the initial price becomes the basis for the negotiation and will influence how much you're willing to pay even after you've had a chance to consider other factors or do research on fair prices. Similarly, suppose you're looking for a job and you're asked how much you want to be compensated. In that case, your answer may serve as the anchor for future negotiations, especially if your request ends up being lower than what the prospective employer was willing to pay.

Anchoring can affect various aspects of decision-making, from negotiations and financial judgments to risk assessments and personal choices. It's important to be aware of this bias and actively work to minimize its impact and effects by delaying judgment so that you can give yourself time to consider additional information before deciding.

2. Status Quo

Status quo bias is when we lean toward decisions that continue current circumstances. In other words, it has always been that way, so you continue that way. These decisions often are the pathways of least resistance.

Let's say you're considering upgrading your phone. You research the new model and learn it has upgraded features, a sleek design, and significantly higher performance. Yet, the thought of learning how to use the features on a new phone, transferring data, and adapting to changes makes you hesitate. Despite the clear benefits, the small effort required to switch and your familiarity with the old phone keeps you from changing phones. That's status quo bias in action.

This bias extends beyond simple daily decisions like choosing electronics or ordering food at your favorite eatery. It significantly impacts more critical financial, career paths, and health choices. For instance, you may continue to see the same primary care doctor despite her oversight in scheduling several preventive tests simply because she's been your go-to physician for years. Likewise, you might remain with an investment firm that has always guided your strategy, not because it gives the best advice or demonstrates the best returns, but simply because the company is familiar to you.

Understanding status quo bias is crucial because it can prevent us from making choices that better align with our goals, preferences, and well-being. Many people stick with the status quo because it requires less effort than trying something new. This bias also protects our egos since trying new things risks being wrong and facing criticism.

Recognizing this bias in ourselves opens the door to more deliberate, reflective decision-making, encouraging us to weigh options more objectively and embrace change when it serves our best interests. Next time you're faced with a decision and feel the influence of the familiar and known, ask yourself: Am I choosing this because it's truly the best option? Less work? Or am I just sticking to the status quo? This awareness is necessary in managing life's numerous choices more strategically and courageously.

3. Sunk Cost

Sunk cost means making decisions based on previously invested time, money, energy, or other resources that are now irrecoverable despite new evidence suggesting that the cost, moving forward, outweighs the benefits. For instance, you've bought tickets to a concert, but on the day of the event, your weather app says that a massive storm with life-threatening winds and snow will arrive. You risk your life and go to the concert anyway, thinking, "I paid a lot of money for these tickets; I can't let them go to waste." The money you spent on the tickets swayed your decision to the potential detriment of your safety and well-being. The money has been spent already, and nothing will change that fact.

The sunk cost fallacy leads people to make irrational decisions, letting past investments dictate future actions rather than making choices based on what would be most beneficial moving forward.

Many years ago, it was discovered that for humans, the fear of loss far outweighs the desire for gain. This is our old friend, risk aversion. Sunk cost bias is a form of risk aversion.

In the stock market, an example of the sunk cost fallacy is when someone continues to hold onto a declining stock because they've already invested a significant amount of money in it, despite clear signs that the stock's value is unlikely to recover. They avoid selling so as not to "waste" their initial investment, even though selling and reallocating the funds to a better-performing stock would be wiser.

To overcome the sunk cost fallacy, it's helpful to recognize that the past expense or investment of time, money, and energy cannot be recovered and should not influence future decisions.

Remember, it's not about what you've already spent; it's about what choice serves you best from this moment forward. Letting go of sunk costs can free you to make decisions that align more closely with your goals, well-being, and personal growth.

4. Confirmation Bias

This is when you unconsciously or consciously seek information that supports the view you're already leaning toward. It causes you to undervalue relevant data, or not be willing to hear a second opinion. This bias can skew your perception and lead to choices based on unbalanced information.

Imagine you're considering selling a new health supplement line in your chain of grocery stores. You decide that you are going to add mushroom gummies. You then look for articles that support your decision. In fact, you come across a handful of glowing reviews and articles about mushroom gummies. Then you discover a much larger number of mixed or negative reviews—which you now dismiss. You decide that the positive articles are more accurate and add the new supplements. This is confirmation bias: you've given undue weight to the positive feedback that aligns with your desire while neglecting a potentially more representative range of experiences.

Combating confirmation bias requires you to actively seek out and consider a broad spectrum of information, especially evidence that contradicts your initial assumptions or preferences. It's about being open to changing your position based on a comprehensive view of available evidence rather than cherry-picking data supporting your beliefs. This open-minded approach leads to more informed decision-making and advances a mindset that values curiosity, flexibility, and a willingness to be guided by a fuller understanding of the facts.

5. Framing Bias

This is another form of cognitive bias in which your decisions are influenced by how options are presented, either with positive or negative connotations. The framing or portrayal of information affects your choices more than the actual content of the options. This bias highlight that the phrasing and context of information can significantly shape your perceptions and decisions.

Two examples of framing bias:

1. **Healthcare Decisions**: Imagine a doctor explaining surgical treatment options to a patient. The doctor could say, "This surgery has a 90% survival rate," or "There is

a 10% chance of death from this surgery." Although each statement presents the same statistical fact, the first, with its positively framed 90% survival rate, is more likely to be reassuring to the patient and encourage the choice of surgery. The second, focusing on the 10% mortality rate, might scare the patient away from choosing the surgery due to the emphasis on risk.

2. **Marketing Products**: Consider a supermarket that labels ground beef as either "75% lean" or "25% fat." Although both labels describe the same product, consumers generally respond more favorably to the "75% lean" description because it sounds healthier. This positive framing makes the product more appealing than the one that highlights the fat content, which has a negative connotation.

To combat framing bias, focus on the factual content rather than how it's presented and consider the information from multiple perspectives. Actively reframe the situation to understand how different presentations might affect your decision. Additionally, seek neutral opinions from others to gain unbiased insights and ensure a balanced view.

6. Overconfidence

Overconfidence bias happens when you have an inflated sense of your own skills, accuracy, and judgment. This can lead you to take greater risks, make decisions without sufficient evidence, or underestimate the complexity of a situation.

Two examples of overconfidence bias:

1. **Investing in the Stock Market**: This is a common scenario in which overconfidence bias appears. An investor might have experienced a few successful stock picks and believe they have a special talent for timing the market. They then make riskier investments, assuming they can predict market movements better than others. This can result in significant financial losses when market conditions change unexpectedly, demonstrating that the investor's confidence was not as well-founded as believed.

2. **Business Decisions**: Consider a CEO who has led a company through several successful product launches. Buoyed by past successes, the CEO might rush into a new product launch without sufficient market research, convinced of their ability to understand consumer demand. If the product fails to resonate with consumers, the company could face substantial financial losses and damage to its reputation. Overconfidence in decision-making can lead to overlooking crucial research and preparation.

More succinctly, overconfidence bias is remembering the times you nailed it and forgetting the times you didn't. Overconfidence bias can be a critical pitfall in both personal and professional scenarios, making it essential to continually seek evidence and maintain a realistic assessment of your capabilities and the situation.

Addressing overconfidence bias starts with acknowledging it. It's about seeking feedback, considering past outcomes more objectively, and adopting a more cautious approach to decision-making—here's where a little bit of risk aversion will be your friend. It means stepping back and asking, "What am I missing? What could go wrong?" By recognizing our overconfidence tendency, we can make more grounded, realistic decisions and avoid the pitfalls of wearing those rose-colored glasses.

7. Expertise Bias

Have you ever wondered how scammers choose their victims? The pattern of fraudsters often targets individuals who are regarded as experts in the particular field in which they intend to defraud them rather than those who possess only a superficial understanding of the subject. Bernie Madoff was a valued figure in the finance sector and orchestrated a Ponzi scheme that primarily deceived experienced investors, including savvy financial experts and affluent individuals. This former chairman of NASDAQ leveraged his esteemed reputation to build trust and credibility in this large group of well-informed people.

Madoff presented these seasoned investors with opportunities that seemed fail-safe, offering steady returns that consistently outperformed market averages. His reputation and the allure of consistently high profits led these financial professionals to lower their guard. They relied on Madoff's perceived integrity and financial acumen, skirting the rigorous checks they typically performed.

Scammers are overconfident, and their expertise bias leads people to believe that because they are experts in a particular field, they are not vulnerable to being conned. It is precisely their expertise that allows them to be conned.

A journey of a thousand miles begins with a single step, and recognizing our biases is crucial to preventing them from negatively influencing our decisions. Understanding and managing these biases is vital. It calls for honest self-reflection and careful assessment. You can better protect yourself from biases by critically examining what influences your judgments.

Chapter Eleven

——⁓——

Top Six Reasons We Make Bad Decisions

How do you tackle your work each day?
Are you scared of the job you find?
Do you grapple with the task that comes your way?
With a confident, easy mind?
Do you stand right up to the work ahead?
Or fearfully pause to view it?
Do you start to toil with a sense of dread?
Or feel that you're going to do it?

You can do as much as you think you can,
But you'll never accomplish more;
If you're afraid of yourself, young man,
There's little for you in store.
For failure comes from the inside first,
It's there if we only knew it,
And you can win, though you face the worst,
If you feel that you're going to do it.

Success! It's found in the soul of you,
And not in the realm of luck!
The world will furnish the work to do,

But you must provide the pluck.
You can do whatever you think you can,
It's all in the way you view it.
It's all in the start you make, young man:
You must feel that you're going to do it.

How do you tackle your work each day?
With confidence clear, or dread?
What to yourself do you stop and say
When a new task lies ahead?
What is the thought that is in your mind?
Is fear ever running through it?
If so, tackle the next you find.
By thinking you're going to do it.

How do you tackle your work each day?
Are you scared of the job you find?
Do you grapple with the task that comes your way?
With confidence, ease of mind?
Do you stand right up to the work ahead?
Or fearfully pause to view it?
Do you start to toil with a sense of dread?
Or feel that you're going to do it?
What is the thought that is in your mind?
Is fear ever running through it?

If so, tackle the next you find.
By thinking you're going to do it.
—Edgar A. Guest

> *"You need to remember that your excuses are seducers, your fears are liars, and your doubts are thieves."*
> *(Robin Sharma, 5 am club)*

As discussed in my previous book, *Training Your Mind for Split-second Decisions*, we make about 30,000 to 35,000 daily decisions. Most of these are mundane and have minimal impact—what to wear, what color shoes to wear, what news program to watch, etc. However, a substantial number of those daily decisions impact our lives profoundly. Hence, understanding the dos and don'ts of decision-making is essential.

We've discussed five main factors that can negatively impact our decision-making. However, one of them is so pervasive and insidious that if it is not confronted and then crushed, your fast decision-making ability will be weak, and your ability to have a successful personal and professional life will be compromised. So, let's talk about fear.

How Fear Can Hinder

We all carry some sense of fear that we have learned. It has been taught to us, forced upon us, and has our experiences. I recognize that life has not always been easy for many people. Perhaps you're not where you thought you'd be. Circumstances beyond your control stifled your childhood dreams. You didn't ask to be hurt or violated. You did not expect to be let down by those who made promises—your parents, your boss, your coach, the people who were supposed to come through for you. You never wanted to move back home. You didn't intend to hurt that person. You were not ready to lose your father, mother, child, or best friend. She said it would be forever. He promised he would return. You knew you should not have been there. You wanted to go back to school. You did not mean to drink so much. You never expected to get sick. You thought the interview went well. You imagined you would be farther along in life. You have always wanted to be thinner. Fear can be learned and internalized from any situation.

People are born with only two natural fears: the fear of loud noises and falling. All other fears you have learned. Therefore, they can be expunged. You must find out where they lurk—a search-and-destroy mission. How do you do this? Start by sitting down with a notebook and pen, asking yourself, "What do I fear?" Now, write down the first three things that come into your mind.

Next, wake up early in the morning—four or five a.m. This is when your mind is most serene. Reflect and identify more fears. Consider especially what you are worried others might discover about you. Write down three (or more) things that come to mind. There you have it—more fears identified.

Keep the process of overcoming fear as straightforward as possible. Often, simply being able to name fear is all you need. If a particular person causes you to fear, remember that you do not have to confront them unless it truly serves your best interests. The key is to address the fear you have allowed that person to create without involving them. Only you can determine what it will take to move beyond your fear.

How do you minimize, destroy, or move past fear:

1. Identify and acknowledge it

2. Confront it!

3. Be super selfish and shift your perspective to one that serves you.

4. Talk to yourself through self-talk.

5. Force yourself to move past fear. Courage is the ability to move past fear. Be courageous for yourself. The only thing that can really hurt you is you.

6. If possible, forget about it by overwhelming your fear with other memories.

The practical perspective about fear is that it is a powerful, natural, and primitive emotion triggered when we perceive real or imagined danger. It is a key survival tool that prepares our body to face threats through the "fight or flight" response. When a person experiences fear, several physiological changes occur in the body, driven by the amygdala, a part of the brain responsible for processing emotions. And thousands of years ago, in a primitive period, fear was necessary. Fear could also be called "heightened awareness" because it could protect you from predators trying to eat you. While that is not the case anymore, the physiologic responses that fear causes in you are still active and primed. It activates your sympathetic nervous system, greatly influencing our decision-making, especially when stressed. Here is a brief breakdown of the impact:

❖ **Intensified Alertness:** The increased production and release of adrenaline and noradrenaline sharpens the brain's alertness, priming you for quick decisions. Adrenaline primarily boosts the body's ability to respond to immediate threats, while noradrenaline helps maintain focus and readiness.

❖ **Focus Changes:** This concentrated focus helps in urgent situations by minimizing distractions. However, it can also lead to missed details or broader implications, potentially resulting in decisions that solve immediate problems but create long-term ones.

❖ **Impaired Higher-Order Thinking:** Although you might be faster in responding, stress can impair the functions of the prefrontal cortex.

❖ **Stress Effects:** Frequent or prolonged system activation can lead to mental and physical exhaustion, diminishing decision-making quality over time. Individuals under constant stress might find themselves reacting hurriedly rather than responding thoughtfully.

❖ **Memory Influence:** Immediate memory may improve temporarily to deal with present challenges, but chronic stress can hinder long-term memory formation. Fears' impact on the hippocampus causes poor memory of past events and can adversely affect learning and future decision-making.

1. Confronting Fear

Fear triggers the activation of the sympathetic nervous system, leading to the "fight, flight, or freeze" response. When making fast decisions, freezing is not an option. Overcoming your fears liberates you, enabling you to take decisive action and think more clearly, free from the influence of those biochemical pathways.

And while I use the word fear itself many other words mean fear as well: anxiety, worry, dread, terror, panic, apprehension, unease, trepidation, nervousness, phobia, jitters, agitation, foreboding. People often use the previous words to disguise or not admit to fear. There's a little folktale I heard about the origin of fear:

"Once upon a time, the devil sought a way to control humanity without having to intervene constantly. He pondered deeply, looking for the most effective method to undermine people's lives. One day, he had a revelation: he would create fear.

The devil released fear into the world, whispering doubts and anxieties into the hearts of men and women. Fear began to spread like wildfire. People started to worry about the future, fear the unknown, and distrust each other. They hesitated to take risks, pursue their dreams, or reach out to others. Communities fractured, and individuals isolated themselves, paralyzed by their own anxieties.

The devil watched as fear did all the work for him. There was no need for further intervention. Fear alone was enough to stop people from living fully and genuinely. It controlled their thoughts, actions, and decisions, keeping them trapped in a cycle of anxiety and inaction.

With fear firmly in place, the devil's work was complete. He no longer needed to exert any effort to disrupt humanity as fear continued to do his bidding. The world was now filled with hesitation, mistrust, and unfulfilled potential.

The story concludes with a powerful lesson: recognizing and overcoming fear is essential for personal growth and freedom. Only by confronting our fears can we break free from the devil's grip and live our lives to the fullest."

Author unknown

Fear can be the most destructive and dangerous of all the emotions. It is absolutely essential to take time and control it. What you create should not control you! Your thoughts are creative, and thus, you create fear. Now, control it.

Fear can profoundly impact your decisions, and therefore, it is necessary that you remain vigilant in recognizing its presence. By identifying and understanding your fear, you can consciously minimize its influence and make faster, better, rational, and more informed choices.

Here is a simple and rapid memory aid that you can use to help you recognize when you are experiencing fear:

- ❖ F: Do you feel scared?

- ❖ E: Are you experiencing physical (increased heart rate, sweating, trembling, fearful facial expressions, dilated pupils, or nausea) symptoms?

- ❖ A: Are you avoiding a certain situation or topic?

- ❖ R: Are you seeking reassurance?

If you answer yes to any of the above questions, then fear impacts your decision-making ability. And likely, the more questions that you answer yes to, the more fear you are experiencing. Being afraid means that your fear is stronger than your faith at that time.

Here are the five simple steps that you should practice when confronting fear.

1. **Call it out:** Seek it out and clearly state what makes you afraid.

2. **Assess it- Break It Down:** Consider the possible and more likely scenarios of a situation and a few even worst-case scenarios.

3. **Be honest with yourself - assess likelihood:** Evaluate how probable each scenario outcome may be.

4. **Be your own hero** – Prepare practical strategies to conquer fear – self-talk (no one better, quick breathing technique, meditation, etc.

5. **Visualize Success:** Picture yourself overcoming fear.

Allow me to share a story with you called The *Alps*. The story is told of an old African city named Carthage. A nineteen-year-old leader named Hannibal Barca was the commander of the Carthaginian army.

In the Second Punic War against Rome, Hannibal started north from Cartagena and traveled through Carthage with about 40,000 men and forty elephants, which he transported on giant rafts. He reached the foot of the Alps, a range of mountains. Mind you, he had already battled the Gauls on his way to Rome.

The Alps were 470 miles along the inner edge and 810 miles along the outer edge. The width was 80–150 miles. The area of the mountains is approximately 85,000 square miles. There were hundreds of peaks more than 10,000 feet high. Most passages of the Alps are blocked by snow in the winter. The higher the elevation, the colder the climate. The elephants that Hannibal and his army were traveling with could grow up to thirteen feet at their shoulders and as heavy as 13,000 pounds.

Hannibal and his troops gathered at the foot of the Alps. The soldiers were full of fear.

Hannibal stood before his troops at the foot of the Alps and said, "Behold the Alps!" He fixed their sight on the mountains.

Hannibal said again, "Behold the Alps!"

His troops said, "The Alps."

Hannibal said again to his troops, "Behold the Alps!"

His troops again said, "The Alps!"

Then Hannibal said, "See no Alps!"

Then Hannibal, his troops, armor, and elephants began to climb the Alps and successfully passed through them.

The point is, when you are afraid in your life, it is important to acknowledge it, but do not be overwhelmed by it. Confront it and then move past it. Refuse to be paralyzed. Be relentless. Be fearless. See no Alps and move forward. Pick up and carry your cross and decide. Prepare for battle! Slay your dragon, fear. The cavalry is here! You are the cavalry.

2. Analysis Paralysis

Analysis paralysis occurs when overthinking and evaluating every detail prevents one from deciding or taking action. This state of inaction arises from fear, which drives one to excessive deliberation.

John decided to buy a new car. There were three cars he wanted to consider. However, as he researched more brands, models, and features, he became overwhelmed by the many choices. The more details John thought, the more confused and doubtful he became. Eventually, he was stuck in a loop of endless comparisons and fear of making the wrong choice, leading to inaction and no decision. John decided not to purchase a car and to continue riding public transportation. This is a classic case of analysis paralysis.

Three steps to fix analysis paralysis:

1. Set a deadline for the decision and stick with it.

2. Limit the information. Establish a cutoff date and time after which you will not consider new information.

3. Tell yourself that you will win or learn no matter the outcome. No such thing as failure.

3. Delayed decision

This means simply deciding too late. The delay can render your choice irrelevant or allow someone else to decide first. This highlights that delaying a decision is a decision with potentially negative consequences. As Jim Rohn says, "Indecision is the thief of opportunity."

4. Decision fatigue

Decision fatigue is the deteriorating quality of decisions made by an individual who has made many prior decisions throughout the day or over a prolonged period. All those decisions lead to mental exhaustion or tiredness of the brain. Decision fatigue can manifest as difficulty making decisions, impulsivity, or reliance on default choices.

In a study on decision-making, Shai Danziger, Jonathan Levav, and Liora Avani-Pesso reviewed over 1,000 parole decisions made by Israeli judges. "The study revealed a significant pattern influenced by decision fatigue.

Key Findings:

- ❖ **Decision Fatigue:** Judges were more likely to grant parole at the beginning of the day and immediately after food breaks. The likelihood of granting parole started at around 65% at the beginning of each session but dropped significantly as the day progressed, sometimes to near zero by the end.

- ❖ **Default Decisions:** As judges became fatigued from making repeated decisions, they tended to revert to denying parole. They tended to maintain the status quo when fatigued.

- ❖ **Breaks and Mental Replenishment:** The findings highlighted the importance of breaks. Judges' willingness to grant parole increased significantly after they had taken a break, particularly after eating, which suggests that such breaks help replenish mental resources and improve decision quality

This study underscores the impact of psychological factors on judicial decisions and the importance of structuring decision-making processes to mitigate fatigue. Scheduling breaks and managing the timing of decisions can help maintain the quality of judgments in repetitive decision-making tasks.

The implications and findings of this study can be extrapolated to other areas and industries that engage in consistent decision-making throughout the day.

Here are a few strategies to help mitigate decision fatigue:

a) Prioritize your most complex and important decisions too early in the day.

b) Delegate less important decisions.

c) Take regular breaks.

d) Set a timeline for decisions to prevent prolonged discussions.

5. Consulting unqualified individuals for advice

There's truth to the adage, "Be careful about taking constructive criticism from someone who has never constructed anything." Often, people seek the input and insight of those who do not have the experience or depth of knowledge to be advising. While your friend may be nice, that does not mean they have the expertise to advise you about a matter they know little about.

I had a patient who endured four days of significant chest pain to come to the ER because her friend told her, "Your chest pain can't be related to her heart because you're only 31 years old." The EKG and labs showed that she had been having a heart attack the entire four days and had severely damaged heart muscle as a result of waiting. The friend, who was *not* a health care provider, did not know that the cocaine the patient had been using was a major risk factor for a heart attack, even in her age group.

Be sure that the person advising you has the expertise needed to assist you.

6. Lack of sleep

Sleep can have a tremendous impact on our decision-making. Sleep deprivation negatively impacts our pre-frontal cortex, which is responsible for higher-level thinking and judgment. Additionally, tiredness often heightens our emotional responses, making us more susceptible to negative emotions like fear, stress, frustration, and irritability. Given that up to 95% of our decisions are emotional, this can lead to poor decision-making.

The National Sleep Foundation has reported that just one night of sleep deprivation, being awake for 17 hours, can impair cognitive and motor functions similar to someone with a blood alcohol concentration, BAC of .05 % (.08 % is considered drunk).

If you are awake for more than 24 hours in a row, your cognitive impairment is similar to someone with a blood alcohol level of .1% (this is equal to 5-6 standard 12-ounce beer that contains 4% alcohol for a 180-pound man or 3 – 4 beers for a 140-pound female). Fortunately, the cure for one night of sleep deprivation is to sleep.

Chronic sleep deprivation is even more problematic than cognitive functioning. Chronic sleep deprivation leads to exhaustion. Exhaustion is a state of deep physical or mental fatigue. It's more overwhelming than just being sleepy. It affects both your body and mind on a much deeper level.

Sleep deprivation can impair your ability to make optimal fast decisions. The American Academy of Sleep Medicine recommends approximately 7 -9 hours a night to position yourself to make optimal fast decisions.

Are You Chronically Sleep-deprived? Here's a Quick Self-Test

1. **Do you have difficulty getting out of bed in the morning, even after a full night?**

   - Yes / No

2. **Do you often find yourself nodding off or feeling sleepy during quiet activities, like reading or watching TV?**

   - Yes / No

3. **Do you rely on caffeine or other stimulants to stay awake and alert throughout the day?**

   - Yes / No

4. **Do you frequently experience mood swings, irritability, or trouble focusing?**

   - Yes / No

5. **Do you find that it takes you longer to make routine decisions?**

   - Yes / No

Scoring:

- ❖ **If you answered "Yes" to three or more questions,** you're likely sleep-deprived. It might be time to rethink your sleep routine or seek guidance from a professional.

You've made a less-than-ideal choice. Now What?

People may have said, "I don't know what I was thinking; I wish I could have a do-over." This often reflects the frustration of knowing they had what it took to make the right decision but were hindered by sleep deprivation, decision fatigue, sub-optimal advice, multi-tasking, etc.

While we have spent the last several pages discussing the major reasons people make poor decisions, the most important thing to understand is that no matter the outcome, you possess the ability to decide how you will respond. When you develop the habit of finding something positive in every circumstance, you will increase your overall potential to adapt. With this increased awareness comes a greater vision, allowing you to experience life without fear and make decisions faster, with more focus and fewer distractions. You will have the discernment to focus on what you value most.

Chapter Twelve:

—≈—

Control Your Thoughts and Create Your Future

Every positive thought—every idea rooted in goodness and a desire to bring light to the world—can become a reality. But this only happens when you believe. Belief activates potential, transforming thoughts into outcomes.

In *The Secret of the Ages*, Robert Collier reinforces this truth: "You have seen the sickly persons, who couldn't do an hour's light work without exhaustion, suddenly buckle down when heavy responsibilities were thrown upon them and grow strong and rugged under the load. Crisis not only draws upon the reserve power you have, but they help to create new power."

This power doesn't only emerge in times of crisis—it is always within you. Belief is the key to unlocking it.

> *Belief is not something you lack,*
> *It's something you need to grow.*

You already have faith. When you step outside, you trust there will be air to breathe. When you eat, you trust you won't choke. When you sit down, you trust the chair will hold you. These small but profound acts of belief prove that you are capable of faith. You need to strengthen it and direct it inward.

The Role of Thoughts

Your thoughts shape your beliefs. Negative thoughts, even small ones, can chip away at your confidence. Thinking *I'm always messing up* or *can't do anything right* might seem minor, but these habits of self-criticism create doubt and hold you back.

The solution is simple but powerful: replace negative thoughts with positive ones. The following two exercises will help you reduce negativity, strengthen your beliefs, and shift your mindset toward positivity and growth.

Exercise 1: Replace Negative Thoughts

1. Recall Three Happy Moments

Write down one sentence each describing three of your happiest moments. These can be simple—like enjoying a sunset—or major milestones, like a career achievement. Allow yourself to feel the joy of those moments fully.

2. Practice Swapping Thoughts

Anytime a negative thought arises, replace it with one of your happy memories. The positive thought doesn't need to match the negative one—any uplifting memory works. For example, if you're frustrated about work, consider the excitement of your childhood bike ride or a recent vacation. The main goal is to distract and thus stop the momentum of negative thinking.

3. **Build a Habit**

The more you replace negativity with positivity, the faster it becomes a natural habit. Over time, this practice will reduce the frequency and power of negative thinking.

4. **Expand Your Positive Reserves**

Add more happy moments to your list over time. Create a mental library of positive memories to draw from whenever negativity strikes.

Exercise 2: Recognize Your Strength

1. **Reflect on Past Challenges**

Think about a difficult experience from childhood—when you feared failure or felt overwhelmed.

2. **Ask Yourself, "How Did I Do It?"**

Even if you don't know how you succeeded, acknowledge that you did.

3. **Repeat for Different Life Stages**

Reflect on challenges from your teenage years, adulthood, or recent struggles. Each time, ask, *How did I overcome this?"*

4. **Reframe Challenges as Wins**

Every obstacle you've faced has taught you something valuable and prepared you for what's next. What may have felt like a failure at the moment was a stepping stone toward growth. Difficulties were put here for your good. The benefit is not always immediately recognizable.

Your Subconscious: The Key to Belief

Your subconscious is always at work, regulating your body and storing your beliefs, habits, and emotions. It is also deeply connected to the universal power—what some call God, the Universe, or Infinite Energy.

Your conscious mind is the captain of your ship, issuing orders that your subconscious carries out without question. In *The Power of Your Subconscious Mind,* Dr. Joseph Murphy explains the differences between conscious and subconscious in the following illustration: "The conscious mind is like the navigator or captain of the bridge of a ship. He directs the ship and signals orders to men in the engine room, who, in turn, control all the boilers, instruments, gauges, etc. The men in the engine room do not know where they are going; they follow orders. They would go on the rocks if the man [on] the bridge issued faulty or wrong instructions based on his findings with the compass, sextant, or other instruments. The men in the engine room obey him because he is in charge and issues orders, which are automatically obeyed. Crew members do not talk back to the captain; they carry out orders."

The captain is the master of his ship, and his decrees must be carried out. Likewise, your conscious mind is the captain and the master of your ship, which represents your body, environment, and all your affairs. Your subconscious mind takes the orders you give based on what your conscious mind believes and accepts as true.

"The captain must give the right orders, and likewise, you must give the right orders (thoughts and images) to your subconscious mind, which controls and governs all your experiences" by Rober Collier, *Secret of the Ages*.

The Law of Attraction

The Law of Attraction states that what you focus on consistently is drawn to you. Positive thoughts attract positive outcomes, while negative ones draw negativity. This doesn't mean ignoring life's difficulties—it means controlling your focus. Acknowledge negative thoughts, then release them. Shift your attention to positive, uplifting ideas. Instead of resisting negativity, replace it.

For example, if you're worried about failing an exam, don't think, '*I can't fail.*' This thought only reinforces the fear. Instead, think about a time when you succeeded or visualize yourself confidently completing the exam. Positive thinking aligns your energy with the outcomes you desire.

The idea of the Law of Attraction is connected to the universe. The universe is designed to help you succeed. Every experience—good or bad—is a lesson, a building block, preparing you for what's next. Recognize the power within you to turn every challenge into a win. Start today. Take control of your thoughts, replace negativity with positivity, and step into the reality you want to create. You hold the power—it's time to believe in it.

Gratitude is recognizing and appreciating the positive aspects of your life. It means acknowledging the good things— whether from others, nature, or a higher power—and giving thanks for them. Gratitude isn't just about your feelings; it's about facilitating a mindset that attracts more positivity and abundance into your life.

Practicing gratitude daily shifts your focus from what's missing to what's present, reinforcing a cycle of positivity and fulfillment. It's simple but deeply powerful: the more you recognize and appreciate, the more you invite good into your life.

Daily Gratitude Exercise

Start every morning with this exercise before you even get out of bed:

1. **Identify Five Things You're Grateful For**

   Reflect on five specific things you're thankful for. These can be small or significant, such as:

   - I slept well, and my bed was cozy.

   - The kids are safe in the next room.

   - There's a fresh cup of coffee waiting for me downstairs.

   - I can still fit into my favorite suit.

   - I have lunch plans with a good friend today.

2. **Be Specific and Varied**

   Avoid repeating the same gratitude's every day. Build on previous ones. For instance, if you've already expressed gratitude for your child, express thanks for something specific they've done, like studying hard and doing well on a test.

3. **Feel the Gratitude**

Don't just list things—pause momentarily and truly feel the appreciation. Let it energize and ground you for the day ahead.

The Truth About Your Thoughts

Your thoughts are the seeds of your reality. Positive thoughts energize and inspire you, driving confidence, optimism, and growth. Negative thoughts, on the other hand, are self-critical and draining, diminishing your sense of worth and leaving you stuck. Recognizing these patterns is critical. Reject negativity and fill your mind with positivity—it's the first step to reshaping your beliefs.

Consistent and persistent positive thinking is essential to create the life you want. By changing your thoughts to reflect your desires, you activate the power of your spirit to manifest them. Gratitude is the starting point. Begin each day with intentional thankfulness, and watch as it transforms your mindset, spirit, and life. By focusing your thoughts on what you have and love, you align your mindset and spirit with positivity. This alignment creates a ripple effect, drawing more of what you desire. You often already know the answers within you. Trust yourself. Train your mind to believe that the universe has already given you everything you need to succeed—including the ability to make fast, confident decisions. What's true about thinking also applies to decision-making.

Final Thoughts

I started this book with such a very personal story about my sudden, potentially life-threatening cancer because, from the moment we are born, we are all on a pathway that leads to death. Life's busyness, difficulties, happiness, and joy may allow us to forget that we do not have infinite time. However, you do not. And that is my ultimate motivation for authoring this book. Making decisions faster will give you more time to do the things that bring fulfillment. The decisions made early in the diagnosis added time to life. The diagnosis reminded me of the fragility of life. Without having to make multiple fast decisions, I would not likely be here now writing a book.

As an emergency medicine physician, I am blessed daily to be quickly and intimately steeped in the lives of people I have had no prior association with. The most common question that I am asked is, "What are the craziest things you have ever seen?" I could write another book just on that topic. But the cases that profoundly impact me the most are the patients who left their house in the morning fully expecting to come home later that night. Or the unconscious patient who has a grocery list in their pocket, fully expecting to go to the store as you and I do. And then, as a result of the fell clutch of circumstance, there they are on my stretcher, either fighting for their life or dead. One story from many years ago still stands out.

A 37-year-old woman arrived at the ER with "CPR in progress," meaning the paramedics were performing cardiopulmonary resuscitation. The paramedics reported that they were having lunch at a popular restaurant down the street from the ER when a bystander ran up to them, saying a woman had suddenly collapsed while walking. They instantly rushed to the scene, initiated Advanced Cardiac Life Support (ACLS) protocols, and transported her to the ER.

The patient showed no signs of life on arrival and was not intubated. The ER team continued ACLS protocols, and I intubated her. The monitor showed a shockable heart rhythm, and we defibrillated her, but there was no cardiac activity after the shock. We continued CPR and ACLS protocols, maximizing all aspects of the ACLS algorithm for pulselessness and no cardiac activity. After about 35 minutes, I pronounced her dead at 3:47 PM.

The mood among the staff was very somber, with a few tears shed. The patient was younger than we were accustomed to, and though no one said it, she reminded many of us of our own family members. The paramedics didn't have time to grab her purse, so we had no way to identify her. However, she had her cell phone in her pocket, which was unlocked. I called the last number dialed. A man answered, saying, "Miss me already, huh? What's up, boo?" My heart sank.

I identified myself and informed him that I needed him to come to the ER at Hospital X immediately. The man, who identified himself as her husband—I'll call him Mr. Taylor—asked, "Is everything alright? Where is my wife?" He pleaded for information, but as a matter of practice, providers do not deliver such news over the phone, especially when the family member is close by.

Mr. Taylor arrived within 15 minutes with another family member. I explained what had happened, and the shrieks of pain and hurt that immediately followed were palpable. Mr. Taylor explained that his wife was healthy and had no known medical problems. He had just kissed her goodbye an hour and a half earlier. Several days later, the autopsy report revealed that the patient had died as a result of a sudden blockage of blood vessels to the lungs, also known as a pulmonary embolus.

Mrs. Taylor's sudden death highlights that life is short, and we do not know how much time we have on this earth. It reminds us to live with purpose and urgency. We have no time to waste. Don't waste time on decisions that can be made faster and lead to greater rewards and happiness.

The fast-decision-making concepts in this book provide you with **practical, actionable tools to handle tough situations quickly and accurately**. This proven framework offers a systematic approach to decision-making, enabling you to identify key factors, assess risks, and weigh options with precision. By committing to daily practice and seeking feedback, you will master the ability to act decisively and confidently, even in high-pressure, fast-paced environments.

Every decision, whether successful or not, offers valuable insights that can inform future choices. By adopting a growth mindset and leveraging past experiences, you can continuously improve your decision-making abilities and adapt to changing circumstances more effectively. To do this, you must understand that what much of the world calls "failures" are required *lessons* essential for growth and development—in all areas of life, including fast decision-making. This is where you grow— developing the skills and earning the tools required for great decision-making. More succinctly, you either win or you grow.

Learning the art of fast decision-making requires a combination of mental agility, strategic thinking, and a willingness to learn and grow. You must practice daily. This will improve your decision-making abilities and allow you to seize opportunities and navigate challenges confidently and clearly. By developing a mindset of decisive action, you can reach your full potential and succeed in your personal and professional lives.

There is an amazing cyclical chain reaction: your thoughts influence your beliefs, your beliefs are a measure of your faith, your faith is a measure of your trust in God, your confidence is a manifestation of your faith; your faith communicates with your soul, your soul informs your thoughts. You can enter any phase of this cycle, no matter where you are in life and how old you are.

The prime internal ingredient needed to make fast decisions is believing your decision will give you the expected results. Believing that your decisions will be right comes from believing in yourself, a measure of your faith. Your faith reflects your belief in an all-knowing, ever-present, and all-powerful God. Genuinely believing God is infinitely good means trusting He wants good for you. This includes recognizing that most of what happens to you is for your benefit, even if it doesn't seem that way. Your current perspective might not fully understand how what seems like a challenging situation could be for your own good.

****

Coming Full Circle

Forty-one percent of Americans will face a cancer diagnosis, and every single one of us will eventually walk alongside someone we love who is fighting this battle. This is not a theory; this is not from a book. This is real life—my life.

There is a world of difference between "I may have cancer" and "I have been diagnosed with cancer." I learned this the hard way. When I confided in someone close to me about my diagnosis, their response was, "Eat more vegetables and stop eating meat." Another friend said, "Just drink more water." Their words did not capture the gravity of my new reality. At that moment, what I needed was not advice; I needed to be heard. And the truth was that I was scared of what my new reality would look like.

In my darkest moments, I realized that no matter how much love and support surrounds you, you are ultimately alone—with yourself and with God (or whatever higher power you believe in). My mother's care, my wife and children's love, my sisters' support, my friends' encouragement, and my doctors' empathy—all of it mattered. But none of them could truly feel the weight of the questions haunting my mind: *What if I die? Am I going to die?* When the lights go out and you pull the covers over your head, it's just you and your thoughts.

Knowing how to respond is not optional; it is essential

This is what I wish everyone knew when a friend or loved one says, "I have cancer." It helps to have a clear understanding of the dos and don'ts when someone you care about tells you that they have cancer.

Don'ts:

1. When you hear it, do not talk. Just listen.

2. Do not make it about you.

3. Avoid the automatic "I'm sorry." It often lands as a dismissal—a polite way to close the conversation.

4. Most importantly, do not disappear. Silence and distance hurt more than words ever could.

Do's:

1. Listen. Fully. Be present. Put down your phone. Look them in the eyes.

2. Support their family—they are fighting this war too.

3. Call. Check in. Show up.

4. Pray out loud with them. Remember, "For where two or three gather in my name, there am I with them." (Matthew 18:20)

So now we're back to where we started. After several months, 74 medical appointments, and countless treatments that demanded rapid, high-stakes decisions, I am—by the grace of

God—**completely cancer-free**. But the real victory is this: **I have a deeper understanding of how to walk beside someone in their darkest hour.** This journey has left me with something far greater than a clean bill of health. It left me with clarity and hard-earned wisdom that I can now share with all of you.

Incredibly, something else happened during my cancer journey—God started speaking to me louder than ever before. In that solitude, it was just Him and me. And for the first time, I felt true comfort. I realized I was *never* really alone.

Sure, the things that used to bother me still did—*laugh out loud*. But something unexpected happened. I had always assumed that people with cancer became more patient, that they slowed down and took life at a gentler pace. Yet, I did the opposite. I became *less* patient and moved *faster*.

Cancer reminded me of a truth we all share but often forget: *we don't know how much time we have*. So, I chose to make the most of mine. I spent more time with family and with people who truly interest me. Most importantly, I became intentional about being *useful*—deeply, poignantly helpful to those in need and to my community.

Now, I love more softly and care less about things that don't matter.

I have come full circle… Back to where we started, but this time, **stronger**.

Acknowledgements

This book exists because of moments, mentors, and the many people who refused to let me quit.

To my wife, Angela—your steady presence and belief reinforced the course. To Brooke and Geoffrey, you remind me why speed matters, but love matters more. You all are great children. I absolutely love being your father. And I am a great one.

To my mother, Dr. Linda Varner Mount, who taught me that decisions aren't just about logic—they're about legacy. Your strength and discipline shaped every page of this book. To my sisters, DaNeeka Cotton and Donnaka Lewis—you are proof that excellence runs deep in our bloodline.

To the frontline teams and organizations, I've served with— on mass casualty scenes, in crisis-mode institutions, emergency rooms, disaster zones, and with families facing unimaginable tragedy—you are the reason I know what fast decisions under pressure truly look like. Thank you for trusting me when everything was on the line.

To my Shield Vitamins family, what started as a wellness mission became a health journey. Thank you for your passion, creativity, and grit behind the scenes.

To those who stood beside me across institutions and chapters of life:

- Trinity Health – LaRonda Chastang

- Traffic Sales and Profit – Ronnie and Lamar Tyer, Freddie Ra, and Krystal Taylor
- University of Maryland Medical System – Drs. Rodney Taylor, Mel Vyfhuis, and Phuoc Tran
- Johns Hopkins Medical – Drs. Mohamed Allaf and Ana Kiess, and Nurse Amanda Antonucci
- Hampton University – Big Sister Joy Jefferson, Deans Angela Boyd and Aleczander Whitfield, Patra Johnson, Dr. Barbara Inman
- Howard University and Harvard University – thank you for the insights that sharpened my thinking and expanded my vision.

You gave me the tools and trust to lead at the highest levels.

To Ronnie and Lamar Tyler, Freddie Ra and Krystal Taylor and the Traffic Sales and Profit community, thank you for teaching me that strategy without a soul and economic responsibility limits the necessary impact on the community. You helped me turn a message into a mission.

Creative and Publishing Partners

To my editorial team, publishing partners, and design collaborators—thank you for helping me say it straight, clean, and   powerfully.
Special thanks to *Georgina Chong-You* and *Mathew Sharpe*, whose feedback challenged me to dig deeper and refine every word.

To my research team—thank you for the countless hours of due diligence, detail, and dedication behind the scenes.

Fraternity and Lifelong Friends

To my Alpha Phi Alpha Fraternity, Inc. line brothers—*Tim Cooper* and *Joe Jenkins*—your brotherhood runs deep.

To the friends and colleagues who walked with me, challenged me, and encouraged me—*Kazembe Ajamu, Dr. Robert Giles, Attorney Maurie Benemie, Dr. Juliette Saussy, Dr. Michelle Carter, Chairman Dr. Rodney Taylor, Dr. David P. Bayne*, and *Honorable Rev. Dr. Michael Battle, Sean and Skip*—thank you for your wisdom, trust, and unwavering belief.

This book is more than pages and print. It is a reflection of every conversation, challenge, and moment of belief you have given me.

Because of you, I decide faster, bolder, and lead fearlessly—and now so can others.

And finally, to every reader: I wrote this for you. Life is meant to be lived boldly, decisively, and fearlessly. Trust in you and do so. Your future self will thank you!

Let us make fast decisions—together.

Made in the USA
Middletown, DE
06 June 2025

76654746R00106